THE GOD ASSETS

God's Investment in You And What To Do With It

Nicole Kirksey

God Assets: God's Investment in You and What to Do With It
©2017 Nicole H. Kirksey, MPH, MSW

Notice of Rights
Manufactured in the United States of America. No part of this book may be reproduced, transmitted in any form or by any means—electronic, or mechanical—including photocopying and recording, or by any information storage or retrieval system, except as may be expressly permitted in writing by the publisher or author.

Notice of Liability
The information in this book is distributed on an "as is" basis, for informational purposes only, without warranty. While every precaution has been taken in the production of this book, neither the copyright owner nor the publisher shall have any liability to any person or entity with respect to any liability, loss, or damage caused or alleged to be caused directly or indirectly by the information contained in this book.

Print ISBN: 978-1-945464-00-3

eBook ISBN: 978-1-945464-01-0

PUBLISHED BY:

Heritage Press Publications, LLC
PO Box 561
Collinsville, MS 39325

A God-Sized Recipe for Success!! Thank you Nicole for this book full of helpful examples, tools and ingredients for life. Each chapter has bite-sized lessons that I could relate to and implement right away. Fantastic book! We love having you as a key member of the National Association of Christian Women Entrepreneurs.

Diane Cunningham, M.Ed.
Founder and President
National Association of Christian Women Entrepreneurs
www.nacwe.org
https://www.facebook.com/NACWE/

Nicole Kirksey is a highly educated woman who shares her knowledge with passion on her weekly radio show, Foundational Gifts. Reading her new book, God Assets, was like a window into Nicole's brain where everything is cut and dry and the simplicity behind her depth resonates in a new way. Nicole is serious about using spiritual gifts and talents to maximize the body of God, but in her book she explains why. She leads her reader to the truth of their unique design and empowers them with knowledge, Biblical insight and subtle coaching so that they can apply leadership and grow their gifts to maturity.

God Assets will serve as an asset to any believer who is seeking to be used authentically by God.

Heather Randall,
Author and CEO, Christian Women Affiliate
http://christianwomenaffiliate.com/
https://www.facebook.com/ChristianWomenAffiliate/

Most people follow a recipe when they cook. The recipe offers valuable direction and insights that result is a great meal. In the same way, the GOD ASSESTS Approach offers the perfect recipe for the person looking to activate God's plans for their life.

The GOD ASSETS Approach is profoundly simple and easy to remember. Nicole expertly describes a 9-step process based on the words

GOD ASSETS. Don't let its simplicity fool you. This is a valuable process, offering the reader a robust resource that is filled with practical and proven steps.

In addition, the coaching questions throughout the book, along with the scripture references, encourage the reader to go deeper and take their next steps. Not that a book can replace an actual coach; nevertheless, this book can be a significant resource that will help you coach yourself forward.

Dr. J. Val Hastings, MCC, Founder/President
Coaching4Today'sLeaders, Coaching4Clergy, Coaching4Groups, and Coaching4BusinessLeaders
http://coaching4clergy.com/
https://www.facebook.com/Coaching4Clergy/

Table of Contents

Introduction:	**The Big Picture of GOD ASSETS** 1
Chapter 1:	**GOD ASSETS:** **God's Unique Recipe for You!** 9
Chapter 2:	**God and Faith** 15
Chapter 3:	**Overriding Values** 25
Chapter 4:	**Drive, Desire, Devotion, and Dedication** 33
Chapter 5:	**Abilities and Strengths** 43
Chapter 6:	**Style of Conflict** 53
Chapter 7:	**Style of Leadership** 63
Chapter 8:	**Experiences** 77
Chapter 9:	**Temperament and Personality** 89
Chapter 10:	**Spiritual Gifts** 103
Conclusion	 123

Introduction
The Big Picture of God Assets

We Are Family

Like a very large family of natural brothers and sisters, God's spiritual family looks a lot alike on the outside. We have mannerisms, ways of speaking ("Christian-ese!"), and similar characteristics that identify us as being related to one another.

Also like a large biological family, each of us is unique. We all play different individual roles in a larger, important whole. Some of us are more responsible, and some of us are more entertaining. Some appear to be more mature and others more dependent. Some are more helpful, and others may be more in need of help. Some of these roles continue from birth on, and other roles change over time depending on circumstances. Each of us is emotionally and relationally closer to some than others, but we all need each other.

Every individual child in a big family wants to feel unique, but the competition is fierce! In loving, functional families, there is room for each member to shine in his or her own way, and each member is supportive of the unique standout qualities of the others. In families with more dysfunction, members are encouraged to conform, and their unique aspects are criticized rather than embraced positively.

Members of the body of Christ are individual members of a larger family. Each of us was created uniquely, for God's purposes and by His design (Jeremiah 1:5).

The GOD ASSETS Journey

One day in 1998, at an extremely low point in my life, the Lord led me to read Marilyn Hickey's book, *Know Your Ministry.* The book explains the spiritual gifts listed in Romans 12. God impressed upon me during this reading that He wanted me to share this information with others in a big way. This inspiration gave me an exciting and worthwhile sense of purpose beyond my then-present circumstances. I set about on a fifteen-year study of the spiritual gifts and never grew tired of learning more (and I'm still learning!).

Slice by slice, over time, God led me beyond the standard lessons of the Romans 12 spiritual gifts. He has revealed more information about ways that He has designed people, areas in which we are unique, and some of His rationale and purposes for doing things the way He has.

Here are some of the "slices" that have come to me through my study of Romans 12:

1. **Spiritual gifts** are absolute superpowers! God gave these to us, and He will not take these back (Romans 11:29). Gifts come in infinite combinations. Some people get more, some get fewer, but we all get one main gift and we all have some ability in other gift areas (Matthew 25:14-15; Romans 12:4-5; 1 Peter 4:10). People who understand their own gifts and how these function for the good of the body are performing true wonders through the power of the Holy Spirit. These wonders are for the benefit of all.

2. One of the professional skills I have that I love and cherish is mediation. As a trained mediator, I see how people with different personality types approach conflict resolution differently. I have also learned how people change their approach to **conflict** in response to other people. Some of this is learned through experience, but some of this is based on how God has uniquely fashioned each of us.

3. As a teacher of adults and children, I have learned that a person's **temperament**, as well as their approach to learning, is the best barometer of her/his success. How "smart" someone is often fails to translate directly into solid academic performance if a person's disposition toward learning or the environment is negative.

4. As a supervisor, I learned that each employee brings different **abilities and strengths** to their position. Two people in the same job can be equally successful using different unique strengths and abilities. Solid leaders are able to draw out an employee's strengths for the good of the organization and the people being served.

5. As a CEO and a lay minister, I also learned that each leader has a unique style and approach to advancing their team toward their goals. The most effective **leadership** styles depend on the needs of the team. The best leaders will be able to implement different leadership styles to bring about positive results in their different teams—styles with which they are most comfortable based on their personality and experience, and styles that will take more conscious effort and commitment on their part to maintain.

6. As a life coach, I know that a person's overriding **values** guide the decisions and choices they make. These values usually operate in the background, like an unconscious mind or a computer program. Values can serve as a source of both constraint and advancement toward goals.

7. Laboring as an activist and serving with others in critical roles (crisis intervention, ministry, etc.) demonstrated to me that, while skill can be taught, passion and **drive** cannot. People are either invested in the mission, or they are not. The quality of their work and service largely reflects this level of commitment. (The other significant factors that affect work quality are fear, experience, and whether or not they are "built" for the work they are doing.)

8. **Experience** is a great teacher and a great informer. Every choice we make and ability we have is colored to some degree by our past experiences. More than any other experience I have had, being a mom has taught me this.

9. More than other earthly and personal assets, **faith** and a strong relationship with the Lord can serve as a rocket launcher for a powerful, productive, enriching, enjoyable, and impactful career, ministry, and family role. My experiences as a survivor of a great many adverse circumstances have shown me this important fact.

All About YOU!

But enough about me—this book is about YOU! The information I have learned on my professional, spiritual, and personal life journey has been fascinating to me. I am eager to share what I have gleaned with you so that you can apply it to your own work, life, and ministry for victory!

The Book

Each chapter of this book describes one of the unique ingredients that God has used to create and develop YOU as His own handiwork, for His unique purposes (Ephesians 2:10). He designed each of us with certain spiritual and natural strengths and abilities. He has also given us curious and interesting guidelines for interacting with others and special ways in which each of us responds to challenges. We each have a heart for specific causes and particular groups of people who are in need. The combinations—the recipes, if you will—are endless!

Certainly, God is infinite. Anything we know about Him and what He does, we know only in part (1 Corinthians 13:9). There is a great deal more to YOU as an individual and as a servant of the Lord than the topics covered here. These GOD ASSETS are a good and solid starting point to get you moving on your way to fulfilling your destiny and living a great life in Christ!

The GOD ASSETS

The GOD ASSETS concept has nine (9) components that together give us a unique blueprint for God's call on our life and designated life purpose:

- **G**od and faith (faith)
- **O**verriding Values (values)
- **D**rive, desire, devotion (heart passion)
- **A**bilities and strengths (strengths)
- **St**yle of Conflict (conflict style)
- **St**yle of Leadership (leadership style)
- **E**xperiences (personal, professional, spiritual, relational)
- **T**emperament and Personality (personality styles)
- **S**piritual gifts

While assets are usually considered in financial terms, these can also be people or personal qualities. A true asset is anything or anyone lending significant contributions toward a goal. Positive value for the long term is a key characteristic of an asset.

The list of assets above is given to each of us by God to produce a positive impact in our own environments: our families, our friendships, our communities, where we work, where we minister, where we play, and where we worship.

God's Recipe

> *I am the LORD, your savior; I am the one who created you. I am the LORD, the Creator of all things. I alone stretched out the heavens; when I made the earth, no one helped me.* – Isaiah 44:24, *Good News Bible (GNB)*

God is infinite. While only He is perfect, we are still made in His image. That means that there are infinite combinations of characteristics and resources that He has given to us, and these are all reflective of Him.

God has made us to be interdependent. That means others need what we have, and we need what they have. There are many people out there in your sphere of influence who need exactly what you have to offer and share. Each one of those people is waiting for you to activate your GOD ASSETS. There is no one else who has your unique combination of GOD ASSETS to offer those people who need them at the exact and proper time, in the proper place, and in the right way.

The Emperor and Creator of the universe and all things in it took the time to make each of us with great care, thought, and consideration. He had His reasons for doing so with each of us. He could have made us in any way, birthed us at any time, and given us any set of characteristics—yet, here we are, the way we are. Aren't we each worth knowing and understanding on a deeper level for that reason alone?

> *Oh, taste and see that the Lord IS good* (Psalm 34:8)—and YOU are His good creation!

I imagine God to be this very busy and active mad scientist or a super chef, in His own kitchen, cooking up you and me. He's never in a hurry, but He moves with purpose. He may be frowning with concentration, but He's always smiling because, as with all His creations, this is gonna be GOOD! People who are waiting for you and your unique combination of GOD ASSETS are behind Him, and His back is toward us. We can't see over His shoulder, but later we will be able to know many of the ingredients He used to develop the unique "you" when we experience one another.

I remember an old friend of mine who was a good baker. She was sampling a pastry from another chef. She took her time and tasted the sample with purpose. She was able to identify all of the ingredients in that pastry by taste. That's the work of an expert! (Me, I just gobbled the thing up—it was good!)

Some people in your life will be like my baker friend; some will be like me. Some people who are waiting for you will look for specific ingredients in your GOD ASSETS recipe: a sensitive temperament, experience in a particular area, the way you lead, or specific spiritual gifts you can use to minister to them. Most people, however, will be looking to just "taste and see" what God has done and how He will bless them through you.

God worked hard on the recipe that is YOU. I want you to use this book to take the time to sample the way God has made you specifically and to become expert at identifying when your "ingredients" have been activated for what God is planning.

The GOD ASSETS: God's Investment in You and What to Do With It

Remember that God's plan for you is GOOD, even if tough times may have come your way (Jeremiah 29:10-11).

So, let's get started!

CHAPTER 1
GOD ASSETS:
God's Unique Recipe For You!

Feed Me Something

For someone who loves to eat as much as I do, cooking does not come naturally. I'm less of a producer and more of an end-user. It's not that I'm a bad cook or that cooking is difficult for me; it has just not been my favorite thing to do. The easiest thing I can make is reservations.

Blame it on my parents, that's what I say! I was raised on drive-thru eating. In fact, I am old enough to remember when drive-thrus first began. Before drive-thrus, you would have to actually get out of your car, go into the restaurant, and walk up to the counter to order your pre-made food. You usually sat at a table in the restaurant to eat. Shudders!

When drive-thrus came along, people could order and receive food without leaving their cars. You could pull up to a speaker, roll down your window (and I mean *roll*—with a handle, in a circle, using your shoulder and forearm muscles and not a button!), and scream your order into the "box." The fast-food worker would scream your order back. You would then drive around to the restaurant window with your car window still rolled down in all types of weather, pay for your food, get it in a box, roll the window back up (and I mean roll—it was your workout for the day), and eat in the car all the way home! What an ordeal, but that's progress for you!

Drive-thrus fed me through most of my twenties. I did begin to cook more often when I lived on my own and when I became a mom. (The poor child had to eat to stay alive, and baby food only went so far.) I didn't cook my first holiday dinner until I was well into my thirties, and then it was only under geographical duress. We had moved 1,200 miles away from home, and I couldn't get to my aunt's home for Thanksgiving. I'm still pretty put out about that one, and I am not eager for a repeat.

There's No Place Like Home

Lately, things have changed for me. Over the past several years, I have learned the financial, practical, and emotional value of home cooking. I think about my beautiful teenager and the condition of her arteries. I consider my husband and think about the numbers on his scale. I think about ways I can pour more love into them besides washing their socks and pinching their cheeks incessantly.

I am at a point in my life where I would much rather eat a simple, homemade meal over a drive-thru any day. Even though I'm not the world's greatest cook, everything lately seems to taste much better when it's made at home. I am in the kitchen almost daily, cooking up something. It is...bizarre. I feel like one of those movie characters that slowly morphs before everyone's eyes into someone or something foreign.

I have especially learned the value of recipes! I have a few easy-to-cook concoctions of my own on which I can survive, but over time, my repertoire has expanded with the Internet and the accessibility of recipes for dishes great and small. With some preparation and planning, I am now able to produce a good meal that nourishes my family and, on occasion, friends as well. My food even passes the teenager test!

What makes a great, nourishing meal is the love and care taken to prepare it, and the unique mix of ingredients required to produce the rich textures and flavors of the dishes.

Ingredients of YOU!

I love learning about how and why each small ingredient is so important to the whole of the recipe. I have improved many dishes by adjusting the ingredients in a way that fits my family's tastes and needs uniquely. One false move on a substitution and the whole dish is ruined! My husband's preference is spicy food, and my daughter likes sweet flavors. It's all a delicate balance to keep everyone happy.

Perhaps it is the love and care (plus sweat and worry!) that goes into making a home-cooked meal that makes it better than one that is mass-produced. Maybe it has something to do with the care chosen for each ingredient in the home-based recipes I have been willing to try. Whatever the case, I have developed a true appreciation for what is created from scratch (or, from "scratch-like" ingredients!), for a specific person, at a specific point in time.

> *For we are God's [own] handiwork (His workmanship), recreated in Christ Jesus, [born anew] that we may do those good works which God predestined (planned beforehand) for us [taking paths which He prepared ahead of time], that we should walk in them [living the good life which He prearranged and made ready for us to live].* – Ephesians 2:10 *The Message Bible (MSG)*

The GOD ASSETS: God's Investment in You and What to Do With It

For whatever reason, you may not feel very unique. There are seven billion other people who are alive with us on earth right now, with similar needs, wants, desires, and genetic makeup. Humans all share about 99.9 percent of the same DNA, even those who are very, very distantly related to each other.* Each person is equally important, and it can be hard to believe that you stand out from the crowd.

But that's not the truth. You are not a drive-thru creation, mass-produced for easy access and consumption. Instead, God has made you with precision and loving care. You are created from carefully selected ingredients, designed to develop into an individual "product" for specifically unique purposes. God consistently thinks of you and considers you—you are important to Him (Psalm 139:13-17)!

Uniquely by design, God has put together a recipe and created each of us from scratch. No "scratch-like" ingredients here! God knew that having a bunch of identical people was not going to work for His purposes. We are each the real-deal original version.

Before even beginning your individual recipe, He planned your good works, things He wanted you to do that would benefit other people. He knew how He wanted to use you to bless others, and how He wanted to use others to bless you! He knew what He wanted you to be like before He even began. He decided, in advance, how much and what types of ingredients should go into each of us in order to produce the YOU and ME that He desired.

Recipe of YOU!

The recipe of you is a delicate balance of ingredients. It was with thought and great care that God measured out the exact type and amount of each ingredient you needed. He also knew how much

---

*Highfield, 2002; Smithsonian, n.d.

time it would take for the ingredients to combine and form in their unique proportions in order to complete and develop you the way He wanted you for His purposes.

Perfection cannot be rushed! Some ingredients went in at the beginning; others were added later, as you were re-created in and growing in Christ.

Think about your favorite recipe for your favorite food. What would happen if one of the ingredients was missing or if too much of one ingredient were added and not enough of another? What would happen if you threw all the ingredients in at the same time when they were intended to be added one at a time? Perish the thought! It only works if it is done the "right" way.

What's the right way? The way the person eating it (the end user, if you will) prefers it or needs it to be. If one of my good friends (who is a chef) makes me a cake using soda pop, she knows not to send me anything with root beer in it (yuckums!). If they make cakes with fruit flavor, they know not to send me anything with lemon (insert pursed lips!). Chocolate cakes must be milk chocolate and not dark chocolate, and NEVER German (ew!). There is a right cake for me. It may be different for someone else, but for my purposes, there is definitely a right and a wrong cake.

God is the same way. We each have purposes that will benefit various people, or end users. If those people (our tribe, the people we serve, those in our circle) need a particular type of help and support from us, we need the right "ingredients" in order to deliver the services or supports properly.

God knew in advance who needed you and what assets you needed to help those folks. He also knew from whom you needed help and what type of "ingredients" they would need in order to be helpful to or supportive of you. When He created you as a person (and as He develops you in Christ), your ingredients form from

The GOD ASSETS: God's Investment in You and What to Do With It

God's unique recipe to make you the right "dish" at the right time for the right people.

Filled—and Fulfilled!

We are all most fulfilled when we are walking on the path in the way that God planned for us in advance and when we are doing those good works (and ONLY those works!) that He designed us to do. Discovering the ingredients that God used to create and develop you will give you a clearer idea of the work He designed for you to do, the path He has planned for you to walk, and the great life He has prepared just for you in advance.

Each of us is totally yummy! We are uniquely prepared by a combination of ingredients for the paths He has planned for us to walk and for the good life He has made ready for us to live.

What are YOUR unique ingredients? How much of each do you have in proportion to the others? What types do you have in combination? What's your flavor? Let's look at your GOD ASSETS and see!

Chapter 2
God and Faith

Amber, 26, is a single mother of two children. By nature, she is laid back and cooperative. Amber avoids conflict, and she does not like to take the lead. She loves people, and it is very important to Amber that people like her.

Amber's four-year-old daughter, Emma, is a smart, feisty, confident child who wears her emotions on her sleeve. Amber's two-year-old son, Ethan, is much more "chill." He hangs back and observes before diving into activities, and he always seems to be in a good mood. Parenting her kids alone is a challenge for Amber, but she relishes the responsibility. Her children are her top priority.

Amber is employed at a nonprofit organization. She is passionate about the work that she does, and she tries hard to do a good job. Amber worries about her tenure there, though. Her relationships with Liz, the head of the nonprofit organization, and with Rachel, her supervisor, are a bit strained.

To address the stress in her life caused by responsibilities and conflict, Amber relies heavily on her faith in God. Amber believes that it is her faith that keeps her going, and that God has given her faith to share with others in order to keep them encouraged as well.

The GOD ASSETS: God's Investment in You and What to Do With It

Can you relate to Amber's brief story? What about her resonates with you?

> *You shall have no other gods before or besides Me.*
> – Exodus 20:3 *The Amplified Bible (AMP)*

God's first ingredient in His divine recipe of YOU is your view of Him and the relationship with Him that develops over time in your life.

I usually don't come out of the gate putting a faith stake in the sand. I prefer that people come to know about my faith by the way that I behave and through conversations that demonstrate in Whom and why I put my trust.

This "over time" faith reveal is my comfort zone. Like a slow cooker, or carry-out, or meals made by someone else, I'm sticking to it with every opportunity!

But today, I'm writing a book, a book that God put on my heart. Just like any effort of mine to share a new recipe, I have to take risks and come out of my comfort zone to deliver it. Also like a good homemade recipe, I have to start from scratch.

My Own Faith

I am a Christian. I actually prefer the term *Christ-follower* because my faith is in action at all times. I'm going in one direction and frankly, this life of faith takes work.

I can say, "Jesus is Lord" with my mouth and not flinch or stutter (Romans 10:9; 1 Corinthians 12:3). I have a personal relationship with Jesus as Savior, and I believe in the principle tenets of the Christian faith.

I grew up nominally Christian. I like to say I grew up around church, but not necessarily "in" church. God developed His authentic relationship with me over time, as an adult. (Notice, it was He, and not I, who reached out first. John 15:16! I give God His props always.)

As a young adult, I explored tenets of various religions. I tried my own recipe or "blend" of various religions and spiritualities. That worked fine and dandy until the Emperor and Creator of the universe interrupted my life and made Himself known. You can't un-know what you know or Who you know. So, now I know!

So here I am, with a strong faith in Jesus Christ. It is through this faith and my eagerness for learning and teaching that I have understood God's unique design for each of us.

My Lens

How I view God is how I view everything. He is the lens through which I can see anything. In addition to the advanced degrees, the twenty-plus years of human services practice, and life experience, it is my relationship with God that has revealed this portion of His divine design of His people.

My faith is what has allowed me to see God's divine recipe for you and for me *in the way that I see it*. This is the message that God has given me to share.

Other people will have a different understanding of how and why God designed us the way that He has. That's perfectly fine! God is infinite, and His ways are above ours (Isaiah 55:9). He reveals Himself in ways that we understand and can apply. None of us knows everything God has to say on a matter (1 Corinthians 13:9).

Different Beliefs? No Faith? Other Faith?

I know that not everyone believes the same things. In fact, even people of the same faith are likely to disagree. Jesus prayed that all believers in Him would be one in the faith (John 17:20-23) for a reason: because true unity does not come naturally, and we needed prayer in that area!

So how two Christians view God is likely to be different, based on many things: what they are taught in their faith tradition, how they understand the Creator for themselves, what their own relationship is to the Creator, their experiences with trusting God, what their relationship is to humans who claim to represent God, how they understand the Bible, and even their own temperaments, values, and personal experiences in life.

And then there are people who believe differently than I do—people of different faiths. People who are not Christians also have a faith component to their divine design. What they believe influences the other ingredients in their "recipe" and can be used for God's purposes.

Whether or not people are Christian, I firmly believe that God has a plan and purpose for each person's life. Each of us is valuable to Him—priceless, even. That value is not dependent on anything we've done or anything about us. It is all about Him.

My God is a big God, and He is not limited to ministering to people who believe in Him. He drew each believer unto Himself while we were "yet sinners." Every Christ-follower was an unbeliever in God at some point, or at least followed her or his own way. Yet, as believers, here we are!

As Jeremiah 32:27 explains, God is the Creator, and He rules the world and ALL people in it. There is nothing that He cannot do, and there is nothing that is too difficult for Him. Whatever your belief system right now, I know that it is God's will to have a relationship with everyone, individually (2 Peter 3:9).

Whether or not we are Christians, each of us has all of the GOD ASSETS ingredients, including faith of some kind.

So how does your faith fit into God's recipe for YOUR unique divine design?

Faith Is...

What is faith, anyway? Is it only a belief in God? Let's review some definitions and descriptions of faith:

- Persuasion of the mind that a certain statement is true (Easton, 1897)
- Belief, trust, and loyalty to a person or thing (W. Elwell [Ed.], 1996)
- Belief in the existence of God (Merriam-Webster, 2011)
- Strong religious feelings (Merriam-Webster, 2011)
- A system of beliefs (Merriam-Webster, 2011)
- Firm belief in something for which there is no proof: complete trust (Merriam-Webster, 2011)
- Belief in a code of ethics or standards of merit (Encyclopedia Brittanica, n.d.)
- An obligation of loyalty or fidelity, and observance of this obligation (Encyclopedia Brittanica, n.d.)

Some words that have a similar meaning include:

- acceptance
- confidence
- conviction
- hope
- allegiance
- assurance

- certainty
- constancy
- dependence
- reliance

Some words that mean the opposite of faith include:

- disbelief
- dishonesty
- doubt
- uncertainty
- denial
- skepticism
- suspicion
- unbelief

(Roget's 21st Century Thesaurus, n.d.)

The most perfect definition of faith (in my humble opinion) is found in the Bible:

> *Now faith is the substance of things hoped for, the evidence of things not seen.* – Hebrews 11:1, *New King James Version (NKJV)*

I like to read Scripture in different translations, because each speaks to us differently at different times. Here is Hebrews 11:1 again in some other translations of the Bible:

- Faith makes us sure of what we hope for and gives us proof of what we cannot see. – *Contemporary English Version (CEV)*

- Now faith is the assurance (the confirmation, the title deed) of the things [we] hope for, being the proof of things [we] do not see and the conviction of their reality [faith perceiving as real

fact what is not revealed to the senses]. – *The Amplified Bible (AMP)*
- The fundamental fact of existence is that this trust in God, this faith, is the firm foundation under everything that makes life worth living. It's our handle on what we can't see. – *The Message Bible (MSG)*

NOW Faith!

If you want to see a church start roaring like they're in a football stadium, get some preacher started talking about NOW faith! Faith is for NOW! It's not yesterday's faith, it's about NOW!

For every minute of our lives, for every task, for every step, and certainly to fulfill our calling, we have to have FAITH—faith that what we're doing is what we are called to do and that it will make a difference for good.

Faith: It's In YOUR Recipe!

You can have the best recipe for the best dish ever. You may have made it 101 times. On the 102nd time, you may not have all of the ingredients. You may try substitutions or going without the ingredient, especially if you perceive the ingredient to be inconsequential.

Try it, I dare you! Your recipe may be acceptable without it, but it won't be the best. It will definitely not be the same as the best version.

How you view God is how you view everything. Your faith informs every other aspect of your unique recipe, or your GOD ASSETS.

- Your faith determines your *values*. What you see as important is determined by what you fundamentally believe to be true.
- What you are passionate about and what *drives* you is also

informed by your faith. You can't live for something (or die for it) without a great sense of faith or devotion.
- How you use your **strengths** is informed and determined in large part by your faith, a sense that there is a purpose larger than yourself. You can use your powers for evil or for good.
- How you resolve **conflicts** is based on how you view the worth of other people and by what you see as important. Only your faith and your values can guide you there.
- Your **leadership** abilities and preferred style depend greatly on your temperament and your experiences, but what you do with these leadership abilities is informed by your faith and what you believe to be true and important.
- How you respond to the **experiences** in your life is based on how you view God, your relationship to Him, and the health and strength of your faith. You may view the same experience differently based on how your faith grows and changes over time.
- Your ability and willingness to moderate your **temperament** (internal, natural response) and your personality (the "you" that you show others) comes in large part from how you see your behavior impacting others, which is based largely on your faith and your worldview.
- Certainly, our **spiritual gifts** are given for the edifying—or building up, from Ephesians 4:12—of other believers. How we use these gifts depends on how we view God and how we esteem His expectation of us as stewards. God gives everyone at least one of the motivational (or foundational) gifts in Romans 12. Researchers have observed evidence of these gifts in children, and identical twins raised separately have been observed as having the same gift (Fortune and Fortune, 1987). Whether we use this superpower for evil or for good, God will not take it away (Romans 11:29).

Faith: What Is It Good For?

As an asset, how does God use our faith in our unique design?

- **Fear Buster** – The antidote to fear is faith. When we are in faith, we truly believe that we are able to accomplish all that we set out to do. As our faith is activated, we get into motion toward those things that God is leading us to accomplish.
- **Growth Agent** – As our faith grows, we can accomplish more and more. We may not have had faith to accomplish that great big dream in our hearts before, but as our faith is strengthened, we are willing to go farther and farther toward accomplishing it.
- **Strengthening Agent** – We will have challenging, unpleasant experiences along the way on our road to accomplishment, achievement, and fulfillment. Faith keeps us strong and helps us to keep moving forward in spite of challenges.
- **Light Unto Our Path** – Not sure of the next step to take? Faith will give you the strength and the courage to take a step, any meaningful step, toward your goal or calling, knowing that God will be there to guide you the rest of the way.
- **Condemnation Buster** – Faith keeps our view positive. Even if the moves we make turn out not to be perfect, we know that we can always start anew without looking back and without beating ourselves up.
- **Connection Builder** – Faith encourages us to let others in on our visions, dreams, and plans. These other people can support us in tangible ways and help us get to our goals sooner.

Coaching Questions

- How is your faith different from the faith of those people around you? How is this uniqueness an asset to you and to others?
- At the beginning of the chapter, we introduced you to

The GOD ASSETS: God's Investment in You and What to Do With It

Amber. How might God be using Amber's faith as a key ingredient in His design for her as it relates to work, parenting, and life?
- What are some ways in which you can share your faith and its fruits with other people to inspire, encourage, educate, support, and strengthen them?
- If your GOD ASSETS were the recipe to your favorite dish, what ingredient would FAITH be? Why is that so?

CHAPTER 3
Overriding Values

Your values are your current estimation of truth. They represent your answer to the question of how to live. – Steve Pavlina

We met Amber in chapter 2. Let's meet Liz, the head of Amber's organization.

As a child, Liz had her life all mapped out: graduate degree by 25, marriage by 26, two children by 30. She achieved all of that, but what she didn't plan for also happened—she got a divorce.

As Liz's life was changing from what she had planned and hoped, she saw an opportunity to reinvent herself and her goals. At 32, she quit her high-powered corporate job to start a nonprofit organization that served women in transition.

Working in the nonprofit world did not prove to be the vacation from the hustle and bustle of corporate life that Liz had hoped. She realized that she had to work even harder to be successful. Liz could not build her own success by relying on the assets of her corporation, including its financial strength. Unlike a corporate employee, she could not move from company to company to get ahead. Instead, Liz had to stay committed, and she had to work twice as hard to get half as far toward the goals she set for her organization.

Liz is the CEO and the face of the organization. She loves representing her nonprofit in the community and in the media. It is of great value to her as a person and a professional.

Liz runs her nonprofit much like a corporation. Because the mission is so important, Liz has very high expectations of her organization: efficiency, effectiveness with measurable outcomes, top-quality customer service, workable (yet aggressive) long-range plans, ever-increasing donations, and of course, top-notch employees. Some of these expectations are more theory than practice in small people-serving organizations, where budgets are small and needs are great.

Those employees who are able and ready to serve at the high-standards level that Liz sets tend to experience a great deal of satisfaction in their work. Employees like Amber whose performance is not up to the standards that Liz has set tend to have trouble in the organization—and a short tenure.

Liz's push for excellence is driven in large part by her values.

Values

In the chaos of the world, values bring a sense of clarity and security. They inform us of what is important, what is top priority, and how we should be living our lives.

When your behaviors and choices are in line with your values, you will experience a sense of peace, joy, and affirmation. You believe that how you see yourself and what you're actually doing in action, word, and deed are one and the same. For example, if one of your primary values is love and your behavior demonstrates that you love and care for the welfare of others, then you believe that you are actually who you tell yourself you are. That is a great thing!

Values do not, in and of themselves, refer to morality or lifestyle choices. The concept of your personal values is less about what you *think* is important. That's the "right" answer. Values are more about what is truly and authentically important to us, the "real" answer.

Whether we are liberal or conservative, and regardless of what religious beliefs we hold, we all have values—beliefs of what is essential and things that we hold dear.

The Value of Values

You feel most authentic, alive, effective, and at peace when your work, life, decisions, and behaviors are fully aligned with your core values.

Knowing your core values* helps you to:

- **Fulfill your potential.** There is power in naming your values out loud and in living these out day to day. Core values help define who you truly are and how you are unique. Putting your values in action through work and ministry helps you to share these values with other people. Sharing your values through service helps you to learn more about yourself in the process. You develop a sense of responsibility for your choices, behavior, and successes because you have guidance and support from your values to help you.

- **Make better decisions.** Some decisions are good. They are the ones that work for *you*. Some are "right" because they're based on expectations or a vision or plan you may have. Other decisions are "best" for you because these actually align not so much with what you want, but with who you are. The decisions that are best for you may not be the decisions that are best for others because the "who" of who

---

*(Brownson, 2010; Brownson, 2013; Johnson, 2011).

they are is different from the "who" of who you are. You can use your values as a guide to help you make the best decisions for yourself and, as appropriate, the best decisions for others.

- **Simplify.** Knowing your values can help you weed out those activities that do not align with what is truly important to you. For example, if you truly believe that family is a core value of yours, then many of the activities you choose should reflect building relationships with your family members and spending a relatively high quantity and quality of time with them. It doesn't mean that "me time," "girlfriend time," and "man cave time" should not exist. It just means that these should not be top priority in comparison to quality time with family members if building family is truly a top value. Simplifying means spending more time on things that honor your values.

- **Focus.** If simplifying can be compared to adding, focus is like subtracting. If you want to focus on your value of faith, for example, you need to remove those investments of time, energy, talent, effort, and money away from efforts that do not reflect the principles of your faith. Spend less time on things that do not honor your values.

- **Identify what's missing or lacking.** Knowing what your primary values are can help you to pinpoint which of these you have been delaying or neglecting in your work, ministry, or activities. Think of ways that you can make changes that integrate more of these core values into your day to build more of a sense of genuine fulfillment.

- **Feel in charge and in control.** Making sound decisions based on how these line up with your values gives you a genuine (and accurate) sense that life is not just haphazardly happening to you. This allows you to see that you have a sense of agency in your life and that you are taking full responsibility for it.

Values and Coaching

As a life and leadership coach, one of the first activities I do with a person I'm coaching is to help her identify her core values. Knowing these values helps me to support the client in making the decisions she will need to make for herself during our coaching relationship. Helping my clients identify their core values and align with these is among the most important supports I can offer as a coach. It is more important than any problem I can help them solve or any personal "ache" I can help them remedy.

I take my clients through exercises that not only identify their values, but that help them to understand how these are present or activated in their lives. From this process, my coaching participants are better able to coach themselves and resolve issues and conflicts on a daily basis. They don't have to wait until our next session all the time to talk something through—one of the main tools that they need for decision making is right there at their disposal.

In my work with the people I coach, I can help them use their core values to identify what motivates them toward excellence, what energizes them and brings them joy, what de-motivates them and brings down the quality of their work and their environment, what stresses them out and distracts, and the one or two primary things that hold them back from achieving the things they truly want. There is a lot they can tell from identifying their values!

We cannot work together as coach and client to build a recipe for joy, fulfillment, and success without a client's true understanding of his or her core values. It's like baking a cake without sugar, except in this process, there is no viable sugar-free sweetener alternative.

Values in Churches, Organizations, and Businesses

If you Google the phrase "core values," you will see that these are largely addressed in a business context. Companies often define the principles and ideals they operate from or those from which they engage the public. Common core values for businesses are commitment, loyalty, diversity, teamwork, and excellence.

Values define an organization's culture. Progressive, innovative, and family-oriented organizations and businesses such as Starbucks, Ben and Jerry's, Chick-fil-A, Zappos, and Whole Foods are known especially for having cultures that are defined by an explicitly stated set of core values. These values permeate the organization's products, marketing, customer service, community interaction, and profit handling.

Values can be motivating factors, whether we publicly identify these or not. For example, certain types of companies and business are clearly motivated solely or primarily by profit. They have little, if any, genuine regard for the damage that their products and "services" cause to the public. These companies will never put "money" and "self-interest" in their list of core values on their websites, but every decision they make is motivated by these factors.

Core values help organizations and businesses:

- Define acceptable behavior
- Limit the parameters of product or service offerings
- Establish hiring practices
- Identify an organization's unique selling points and position in the marketplace
- Create a healthy, productive work environment
- Unify the various departments and units within a larger organization

Values cannot be a set of words on paper. These must be believed by all stakeholders, accepted as valid and workable in relationship to the organization's mission, implemented as part of the organization's day-to-day operations, and evaluated as part of performance evaluations for employees and the organization as a whole.

The same way that core values help organizations and businesses, they help people to:

- Define acceptable behavior
- Limit the parameters of the types of services or work they perform
- Establish associations with particular people
- Make people unique within the body of Christ, and within the organizations and communities they serve
- Create healthy, productive environments wherever they are
- Connect with people in other parts of the body of Christ and organizations who would otherwise remain strangers

Coaching Questions

- As an asset, how does God use values in our unique design?
- If your GOD ASSETS were the recipe to your favorite dish, what ingredient would your Overriding Values represent? Why is that so?
- Do you believe that your life is now in alignment with your core values? (HINT: you don't have to know what your values are to answer this question—use your intuition.) If your answer is yes, name three examples of why this is true. If your answer is no, identify the one main reason why you believe this is not true.
- What information do you need about your core values?
- What steps do you need to take to identify your core values?
- What are you willing to change in your life to insure that your values and your choices are in alignment?

The GOD ASSETS: God's Investment in You and What to Do With It

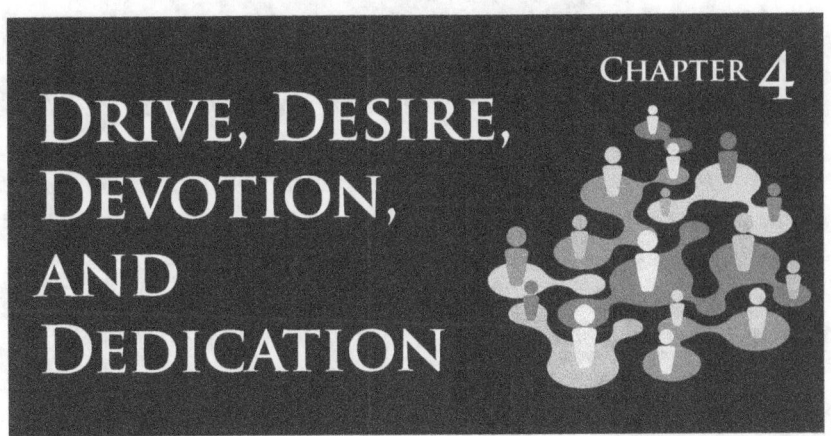

CHAPTER 4
Drive, Desire, Devotion, and Dedication

Both of Liz's children are driven, high achievers, just like Liz and her father, William. Each has areas of passion different from the others and each is motivated by different issues.

At 65, William is the CEO of a Fortune 500 company. He has no plans to step down and retire any time soon. Will worked for twenty-five years at various other employers before landing a directorship at his current company. He worked his way up the corporate ladder diligently and creatively, year by year, sixteen-hour days at a time. Once the CEO position opened up, Will lobbied for it heavily, even though hiring from within was not customary. Since his rise to the top, Will has basically sung the old Sinatra standby: he has done it his way. Driven by an urge to succeed and to do things better than those who have come before him, William remains in his element at the helm of his company, well into the decade when most men his age are eager to retire.

Tyler, Liz's son, is an 18-year-old college student. Although his grandfather was more than willing to pay for Tyler to go to one of the very well-respected universities that had accepted him, Tyler made a bold move and chose to go to community college. Tyler wanted to work and put himself through school. He knew his mother's income would be cut drastically by starting the nonprofit, and his father's child support obligations would end before college. Tyler did not want to be beholden to his grandfather or to put his mother in an awkward position by accepting such extravagant financial support from her father. Inspired by his grandfather, Tyler has been motivated to become his own man and not to rely on others any more than he needs to. He is also determined to set his own course for his career—a career course that his mother and grandfather do not agree with, but one they respect. Tyler is not only driven by a desire to be self-sufficient, however. Tyler's career path and the people he will serve are more important to him than approval from his mother and from his grandfather.

Tyler's younger sister, Madison, is more socially ambitious than career- or education-driven. In that way, she takes after their grandmother, William's wife and Liz's mother. People in the community refer to Madison's grandmother as "Susan the socialite," and Madison is proud to follow in Gram's footsteps. In her sophomore year, Madison is already the co-captain of her cheerleading squad. Her presence on the debate team has made the team cool at her high school. Madison is president of the sophomore class and serves as student council secretary. She chose student council to get connected with the "in" crowd from the junior class—students who are active on the council as well. Her social connection to next year's seniors has been planned for a while. Being popular with upper classmen will expand her social influence! She is as active on the homecoming dance committee as the seniors will allow and spends a great deal of time with her core group of friends. Madison doesn't date, but her list of potential suitors from school and from her grandparents' social circles is growing by the day. Her grades are fine, but Madison's mother worries about the lack of balance she seems to have in her life right now. Madison is not worried. She is fulfilling her passion to serve as an example to younger people, just like her grandmother has served as an example for her. Madison wants to show other teens that life is best when you're excelling in your areas of interest and strength without drugs, alcohol, promiscuity, social media mishaps, and disobeying your parents.

Liz sees her parents in her children and wonders sometimes if this is a good thing.

What's Driving Us?

What is this thing, this asset, called "the D?" As Dr. Phil would say, let's put some verbs in our sentences!

- **Drive:** to carry through energetically; to set or keep in motion or operation; to compel to undergo or suffer a change; to urge relentlessly to continuous exertion; to give shape or impulse to.
- **Desire:** to long or hope for; to express a wish for; to request or ask; synonymous with ache, crave, hunger, thirst, and yearn.
- **Devote:** to conduct an activity of faith (prayer, worship, etc.) in private; to dedicate the use of time, money, energy, etc. for a purpose or cause; to commit; synonymous with consecrating or setting apart for a higher end.
- **Dedicate:** to set apart for a definite use; to commit to a goal or a way of life.

The "D" in our GOD ASSETS is all about feeling and all about action. What is it that we feel that moves our actions into a specific direction?

What's the Deal with the "D?"

Behavior comes from our emotions. What we feel on the inside influences actions we take and impacts our environment or the world around us. These actions express our passions: strong feelings, excitement, and enthusiasm for a cause, issue, or activity.

Among the ingredients in God's recipe for us is some spice and sauce, that special something that gives each of us a unique flavor. In that part of our recipe, we perk right up! If a conversation about our area of passion comes up or an opportunity to serve in our area of passion arises, we are right there, front and center.

The direction of our attention can be for an issue such as human trafficking, abortion, immigration, capital punishment, etc. It can be for a group of people, such as children, teens, women, people living in poverty, the homeless, or other groups. For our interest to rise to the level of a passion (a drive and desire for change resulting in devoted action), both the people and issue components are usually present.

The Flavor of our "D" is HOT!

The more specific our passion focus, the more clear our God-given mission for service is likely to be. For example, caring deeply about what happens to children in general means you have a "heart" for them. Who doesn't love kids, right? That's not "the D."

Drive, desire, devotion, and dedication means experiencing strong emotion and being moved beyond that feeling to actual action. For example, having a passionate desire to see children cured from autism or cancer, and being willing to help with that through regular fundraising and community education, is more specific than just having a "heart" for children. If a person is willing to take these actions, then their desires for a cure and help may likely be an area of passion for them.

For another example, caring about addressing the issue of homelessness is good, but you can be more sure it's an area of passion when your desire to specifically address the homelessness experienced by runaway and throwaway teens captures your attention, your heart, and your commitment. When you are more than willing to work or volunteer at homeless shelters and assist homeless children to find safe shelter and loving support, then that's a greater indication that you are touching on an area of devotion or drive.

Center Stage! The "D" Speaks

Our true passion is a bit self-centered and stingy: it will not share center stage with much else. We think about it regularly, even constantly.

How do you know when you want the best for a group of people or care deeply for an issue on the one hand, and when it is your life's passion on the other? Our passions take a bit of our breath away. These take up space in our minds and hearts that other topics, issues, or interest groups do not. We see ourselves on the forefront of getting things done to address a need, a people, or an injustice, and almost always a combination of the three.

It looks a bit like an obsession, albeit a healthy one. We're always coming up with ideas and ways to respond to the needs or the groups of people in our passion-vision. We have ministry ideas that pop up at random. Ideas about legislation invade our consciousness at inopportune times. Creative ways to make money to address the issue is a common topic of conversation with people who have similar interests (and those whose ears can't get away before we bend them!). We see the issue or the group of people everywhere, even when others seem oblivious. We can usually point to a time in our lives, early on, when the group of people or issue captured our hearts and when things got serious for us in terms of a burning need to "do something about it."

Rev. James Lyles is a friend who serves out of commitment and passion. He has a true heart for disadvantaged youth in the community. Rev. James runs a ministry that provides different types of arts and activities for kids after school and during the summer months. The ministry, "Youth 10x Better," has the mission of "[inspiring] youth to do their best and then develop and perfect that young person's position, passion, and purpose in God's Kingdom."

While most people care about young people, not everyone has a true drive, desire, or devotion to serve them consistently, as a top priority. Rev. James has embraced the calling of the life of a social servant: low pay, long hours, weekends and holidays, constant pitching for financial support, less-than-desirable work conditions, frequent local travel, emotional drains, and sometimes thankless days, weeks, months, and years. He has chosen to forego some comfort and security in his career in order to serve young people who may not have the support they need to grow up and do their best. These youngsters need help focusing on their God-given passion and purpose versus the negative influences in their environment.

Heartbeat

Rick Warren describes our area of passion as our "unique emotional 'heartbeat' that races when we think about the subjects, activities, or circumstances that interest us. We instinctively care about some things and not about others. These are clues to where we should be serving" (Warren, p. 238).

As an asset, God uses drive to reveal our heartbeat—that issue that keeps oxygen and blood flowing through us and keeps us fully alive.

There are certainly times in our lives when we may have said one thing but thought and felt another (Proverbs 23:7). If we are people of integrity, then certainly this is a disconnect. We may have felt "icky" on the inside either for not saying what we truly felt, or for feeling guilty about what we thought.

God is Truth (John 14:6; John 16:13, John 17:17) and He designed us to be authentic and real, just like Him (Genesis 1:27). What we care about passionately is what, who, and how we should dedicate our time of service and impact on the world. (Deut. 11:13; Ephesians 6:6). In service, we should always "keep it real."

Some questions to ask yourself to test to see if an area of concern or a "heart" issue is a true passion:

- Who do you care deeply about serving (the population or group)?
- What specific concern, need, or area of justice do you think is important to address for this group of people?
- When would you like to help, or when is it important to help? (If NOW is not the answer, it is not your area of passion.)
- Where are the ministries, services, or supports most needed? (This will give you an idea of where in the body of Christ, where in the community, or where in the world you are being called to serve.)
- How should people help? (If money is the only way that the problem can be resolved or the only way that you can see that people can be helped, then this is not likely to be an area of passion, drive, desire, or devotion.)
- Why is this important? (If there is a tendency to defend the importance of this issue in comparison to other equally important groups of people or issues, then it is likely an area of passion.)

An area of passion for me in terms of service is advocacy for abused women and children. When I was a nineteen-year-old college junior, God gave me an epiphany that I was to be a crisis counselor. This revelation came while I was on a family vacation, completely unbidden and out of the blue! That vision drove me for the next two years. This goal determined my major and all of my community activities. After graduating from college, I searched for work at a rape crisis center in southern California (because, hey, Hollywood needs counselors just like the Midwest does!). I worked as a survivor advocate for about twenty years.

I remember living in an apartment next to some particularly loud neighbors, a jerky guy and his invisible (but audible) girlfriend. I had to ask them more than once to turn down their music and to stop talking so loudly. They got on my last nerve, frankly.

One night, the music was off and the loud talking turned to yelling. Through the walls, I could hear slapping and punching. I wanted to be sure that I had heard what I had heard. I hoped I was just hearing a beating in my head because, as an advocate, I tended to "see" abuse everywhere.

But it wasn't in my head. I could hear the girlfriend telling the boyfriend to stop hitting her—first demanding and then asking. I didn't want to wait until her pleas turned to begging, so I went to their door, alone, with my nightgown on (a boldness that comes from being twenty-something and more than a bit naive).

I pounded on the door. When the abuser came to the door, I demanded to see his girlfriend. She wouldn't come to the door. I yelled in to ask her if she was okay. She spoke back clearly, but softly, that she was. I got the feeling that calling the police in that moment would not help to make her safe, that my presence was enough to stop the beating for that night. I said to him, "You and I argue about the noise and that's cool, but this is not an argument we're having. I will call the cops on you in one second if I hear you hurting her again." All was quiet that evening.

I told one of my best friends (a church leader) about the incident. She responded, "You can't save the world." I was dumbfounded (and, trust me, I don't get dumbfounded). She didn't admonish me for potentially putting my life at risk. Instead, she was basically saying that the beating was not important enough for me to jump in it. She proceeded to tell me how some women liked that and put up with it. She went on and on with victim blaming. I was floored. At least I now know that abuse of women was not this person's area of drive and passion!

A few months after the neighbor incident, I was snatched out of a great sleep one morning by the sounds of police radios and talking outside of my window. There had to have been three police cars blocking the street with lights flashing and twice as many uniformed officers outside, plus calls for backup on a very loud walkie-talkie system. I asked the officers what was going on. They said that my neighbor had beaten his girlfriend very badly, and she was injured. Someone had called the police, and the assailant had taken off on foot. The police blockade was there to search for him, a fugitive.

I was not the "someone" who called the police that night. In fact, I had not heard one sound out of them since our previous confrontation. Whoever called the police for her did not save the world, but they may have saved that woman's life that night.

Can you see the spice and sauce in my personal GOD ASSETS recipe? I had dedicated my career to serving women and children who were abused. I sacrificed income, safety, and creature comforts in a work environment in order to impact a cause and a people. (There was no cushy office for me! Only outdated equipment, torn/dirty furniture, and rough neighborhoods.) A problem arose in my area of passion, and I was there, front and center. I spoke out often in the media and at national and local conferences on this issue. To me, it was the most important issue to humanity.

Let your "D"—that spice, that heartbeat, that passion—be a light that shows you the way to ministry and service. It is an asset!

Coaching Questions

- *Where* is my passion? Is there a specific location in the body of Christ, in my community, in my organization or workplace, or in the world that I would love to serve?
- *Who* is my passion? Is there a group of people who I want to help in particular? For whom does my heart bleed? To whom

would I give the last that I had to help, other than my own family members?
- *What* is my passion? What makes me angry? What makes me sad? What is the most important social, political, health-related, or religious issue that needs to be solved?
- What's my first step?
- What's my next step?

CHAPTER 5
Abilities and Strengths

> *He has filled them with skill to do all kinds of work...* – Exodus 35:35 *New International Version (NIV)*

Nobody throws a party or fundraising event like Mrs. Susan! Liz's mom, Susan, makes every guest feel as if they are a person of honor, even in a room of hundreds of people. She knows the value of a handwritten thank-you note and of having lunch regularly with people who matter to her—not only for what they can do for her social calendar, but for how she can help them in the ways that they need. Everyone loves her.

Susan and William's other daughter, Jennifer, recently earned her Ph.D. and is teaching at a local university. No one can handle scientific material and explain it to non-scientific people as well as Jennifer does. Her personality is not as big and bubbly as her mother's, and her skills and interests differ completely from her mother's. Susan and William are very proud of Jennifer and how she is using her own unique abilities for the betterment of others.

To Susan and William, Jennifer's boyfriend, Jason, doesn't seem to have a particular skill or any abilities of note. He's a waiter at Jen's favorite restaurant, which is how they met. Jen's parents are not impressed, but Jen is. She is drawn to Jason's ability to calmly and peacefully respond to any challenge and to solve problems on the fly. His tips are consistently the highest at his restaurant, and the customers frequently note his name on the written feedback about their positive experiences. Like Jen's mom, Jason is extremely hospitable, one of the many reasons that Jen is drawn to him.

Rise to the Top!

If God were baking a cake of you, your strengths and abilities might be the leaven that makes your particular cake rise. Yeast, baking soda, and baking powder are three different types of leaven.

- Yeast is a fungus, and it converts other recipe ingredients into gases to make the cake rise.
- Baking soda has many uses outside of baking, but it must be mixed with other types of ingredients or it will make your cake taste bitter or even soapy.
- Baking powder already comes mixed, or you can mix your own. Again, it relies on other ingredients to be most useful. (Cookthink, LLC, n.d.)

Each of us might have a different leaven based on what's in the rest of our cake and how we're cooking. Your abilities help you rise to the top and to help others do the same!

Able

You have abilities in many different areas of life. For example, abilities can be physical and mental (Ecclesiastes 10:10) or artistic and creative (2 Chronicles 2:7).

Certainly, some of us have more abilities in certain areas than others. For example, my handsome and capable husband would say that he can't dance worth a lick. However, he is a wonderful and creative poet.

In other cases, many of us have abilities in the same area, but they are expressed differently. Two people may have artistic abilities, but one is a painter and one is a poet. The poet can't paint a stick figure, and the painter wants to color her words!

In order to accomplish what He desires, God uses people with all types of skills, abilities, and strengths to serve (1 Chronicles 28:21). The reason that you even have the abilities and strengths you do are so that these can be used for His glory. The reason you have strengths and abilities in one area and not as much in another is because God needs you to serve and offer with what you have and let others serve and offer with what *they* have.

You can expect to have areas of responsibility that match the abilities that you have already (Matthew 25:15). Especially as adults, we should expect to do *more* of what we're good at and less of what we're not as great at doing. Do NOT waste a whole lot of time serving and offering in areas in which you're not particularly strong, talented, or gifted.

Our natural abilities get stronger with experience and by regular use. If you're not using your strengths and abilities regularly, these may wane. In addition, you may not be able to move forward or up to the next level of service.

As your abilities increase, you can also expect that your areas of responsibility will increase (Matthew 25: 20-23). For example, a person may start work as a secretary. He (yes, there are male secretaries!) will learn administrative skills on his job. As his skills build, he should expect to have increasing responsibilities on the job. He may even be asked or expected to teach other secretaries how to improve their administrative skills.

The GOD ASSETS: God's Investment in You and What to Do With It

We Gotta Stay Humble!

People of faith often deny that we have abilities, strengths, and talents in certain areas. We are careful not to get a "big head" and think more highly of our abilities than we should (Romans 12:3). We don't want to fall flat on our faces by relying on our own natural abilities or the flesh (Psalm 146:3). We don't want to be punished or embarrassed by bragging on ourselves (Isaiah 10:12-14). We want to always be sure to practice humility and to give all proper credit for power, success, and might to the Lord (Isaiah 10: 15; 1 Corinthians 4: 7-8; Psalm 115:1).

That does not, however, let us off the hook from using our natural strengths and abilities to serve the Lord and others and to find fulfillment in our work! You don't have to brag about your singing, writing, speaking, or organizational abilities in order to use these effectively. There is nothing wrong with being confident in your competence. Fear, false humility, and confusion are not of God and should not be embraced in any area, especially where you're strong!

Examples of Strengths, Talents, and Abilities

Samson had a job and a rule to follow even before he was born (Judges 13:5). As he grew up, God blessed him and moved in and through him. At various times, God would supernaturally empower Samson to do physical feats that no one else could do. While Samson was arrogant and not the best steward of the abilities God had given him, he did serve and fulfill God's plan. In the end, Samson used the physical strength that God gave him to conquer an enemy, even when that meant his own destruction as well (Judges 13-16).

We do see that Samson's strength was supernaturally empowered and not just a natural ability; however, it was a strength that no one else had. Talents and skills are that way. Usually, people around us do not have the same set or level of abilities that we have. The reverse is also true. We can look around us and see people who have many talents, abilities, and strengths that we don't have, at least not to the same degree.

When King Saul was battling demonic spirits, he sent for someone who was *skilled* at playing the lyre (a musical instrument). A servant referred him to a young man named David, the same David who would later have Saul's job. Again, David's playing ability was empowered by God, but his was the only name that came up when Saul was looking for someone with an ability (1 Samuel 16:14-23).

As an asset in His design, God uses our strengths, skills, and abilities to get jobs done. A lot of strengths are outlined in the Bible. Here are a few:

- Esau was a skillful hunter (Genesis 25:27).
- Tabernacle workers were to be skillful in their artistic trades (Exodus 26, 28, 31, 35, 36, 38, and 39).
- Judah was the strongest of Israel's sons (1 Chronicles 5:2).
- The sons of Reuben, Gad, and Manasseh were notable as highly skilled battle warriors (1 Chronicles 5:18).
- The chief of the Levites was skillful in song (1 Chronicles 15:22); instrumental musicality was also considered a skill (2 Chronicles 34:12).
- Knowledge, understanding, and business acumen are mental skills (2 Chronicles 2:12-14).
- Creative writing is a skill (Psalm 45:1), as is public speaking (Isaiah 3:3).
- Being able to wail the loudest at a funeral is one unique biblical ability (Jeremiah 9:17). I know some candidates for this one!
- The ability to kill and destroy is a skill and a strength (Ezekiel 21:31).
- Being knowledgeable and quick to understand (or plain, all-around smart) is a strength (Daniel 1:4).

What all of these biblical strengths, skills, and abilities have in common is that there was a need for them in the community at a certain time, and God raised people up who had the ability to fulfill those needs out of their particular areas of strength. God is the same yesterday, today, and forever. He does the same today—raises up people with strengths and abilities that are needed for today.

Build on Who You Are

> [E]ach person has greater potential for success in specific areas, and the key to human development is building on who you already are – (Rath, 2007, p. 8).

From the time we are small, we are taught and encouraged to work on improving our shortcomings. If we get poor grades, we are told to study harder in those areas. If we are not good at sports or the best at music, we are told to practice more. When we get to the workplace, our annual reviews are often about what we have not done or what we need to do better. When we get called to the boss's office for "feedback" or "coaching," it is not usually for the stellar job that we've been doing.

Certainly, we should all strive for a basic level of proficiency in all areas of responsibility that we have. However, we are most successful when we are working in our strengths zone—those areas of natural strengths, abilities, and talents that come most easily to us—where we can produce the fastest and most lasting results.

How Do I Find Out My Strengths?

Glad you asked! I recommend to all of my coaching clients to start with StrengthsFinder.

StrengthsFinder 2.0 is an assessment by Tom Rath that helps people uncover their talents. The StrengthsFinder assessment is the culmination of over fifty years of work by Donald O. Clifton, Ph.D., generally known as "the Father of Strengths-Based Psychology."

Scientists in the 1990s interviewed more than 100,000 people from various professions and looked for patterns in the interview data that described the things that people did well and correctly. From this research, they developed a list of thirty-four natural talents that are independent of education, training or skill.

The StrengthsFinder assessment asks 177 questions on a continuum and gives test takers twenty seconds to answer each question. From there, the top five strengths or talents of the test takers are identified from the list of thirty-four (Gallup, 2013).

Talents are undeveloped, raw material—unsifted flour in our recipe, as it were. The goal of the research was to identify these areas of raw, natural talents so that these could be developed into true strengths. Strengths are natural talents that have been honed and practiced over time so that these specific activities are performed at near-perfect levels consistently.

This development of strengths takes hard work, focus, and practice, "much like it does to build physical strengths" (Rath, 2007, p. 19). When you multiply your natural talents with an investment of time and effort spent building knowledge, developing skills, and practicing, you will then have a true strength.

Each of the thirty-four strengths identified in the Clifton research can be separated into one of four domains:

- **Working Harder** (*Striving* in personal strengths; *Executing* in leadership strengths) – Strengths in this domain are about implementing, making sure that things get done.

The GOD ASSETS: God's Investment in You and What to Do With It

- **Working Smarter** (*Thinking* in personal strengths; *Strategic Thinking* in leadership strengths) – Strengths in this domain focus on information gathering, analysis, and casting a vision for the future.
- **Influencing Others** (*Impacting* in personal strengths; *Influencing* in leadership strengths) – Strengths in this domain are used to ensure that ideas are heard and "sold" to others.
- **Relating with Others** (*Relating* in personal strengths; *Relationship Building* in leadership strengths) – Strengths in this domain are about creating and maintaining a functional, supportive team.
(McGinnis, 2007; McGinnis, 2009; Reveal Ventures LLC, n.d.)

As your natural talents and abilities are different from others, so is your performance demonstration of your strengths. For example, there is a strength called Learner. You may have a group of people who are naturally talented as Learners. There are several different learning styles, so each person will express their Learner talent differently. People also have different temperaments, and expressing talents will look differently with different types of personalities.

For a list of all of the strengths themes and the domains these fall under, visit http://cliftonstrengthsfinder.blogspot.com/2007/01/strengths-finder-themes-categories.html.

To take the Strengthsfinder test, go to https://www.gallupstrengthscenter.com/Purchase/. You can take the test online for under ten dollars to identify your top five strengths, or you can invest more and learn the relative strength of all thirty-four of your strengths.

How Should We Use Our Natural Abilities?

- Willingly (Colossians 3:23)
- In the open (Matthew 5:14-16)

- Exponentially (Matthew 25: 14-30)
- Faithfully (1 Corinthians 4:2)
- With expectation (Colossians 3:24-25)

When we do well, we should expect a reward. It may not be the reward that we would choose, and it may not be of immediate and direct benefit to us as individuals, but we do know that a positive outcome will result from proper use of our abilities. We should also be aware that when we misuse our abilities in ways that they were not intended or for dishonest gain, the outcome will be negative.

The Saddest Story Ever

False modesty, fear, lack of opportunity, oppression, and a variety of factors keep people from experiencing the fullness of their abilities, passions, and talents. In the book *Strengthsfinder 2.0*, author Tom Rath states that, "Far too many people spend a lifetime headed in the wrong direction. They go not only from the cradle to the cubicle, but then to the casket, without uncovering their greatest talents and potential" (p. 30).

Do NOT be this person! Use every resource that God has given you (including your talents, abilities, and strengths) to maximize service to Him, to help the most people, and to enjoy the work you do in every area of your life.

Coaching Questions

- What do I know I'm good at doing?
- What do others say I'm good at doing?
- What do I do well with little effort?
- How can I turn my abilities into strengths?
- In the recipe that is me, what kind of leaven might my strengths be? Why is that so?

The GOD ASSETS: God's Investment in You and What to Do With It

Chapter 6
Style of Conflict

Rachel is a supervisor at Liz's nonprofit organization. Rachel directly supervises Amber, the single mom we met in chapter 2.

Rachel is a highly competent professional. She does what is expected of her exceptionally well. She does not understand how and why other people seem to struggle with meeting the expectations of their position.

Generally speaking, Rachel is very straightforward in most matters. While she does consider the feelings of other people, she is not averse to having direct and honest conversations, naming conflicts that exist, and doing the hard work of reconciling conflicts, if it is possible.

Most people do not share Rachel's perspective and would rather deny or avoid conflicts as much as possible. At best, people want to say what they have to say and get the whole thing over with. Rachel does not agree and thinks relationships are healthier after a few rounds of successfully working through conflicts.

Supervising Amber has proven to be a challenge for Rachel. Rachel appreciates Amber's compassion for the people they serve, and her eagerness to do a good job. Amber, however, has some performance issues that need to be addressed. Every time Rachel tries to speak with her about these, Amber quickly ends the conversation, shuts *down, or starts crying. None of these responses deter Rachel. Amber's performance issues and the conflicts between them continue, which frustrates Rachel.*

Rachel has discussed Amber's performance issues and her reluctance to problem-solve with Liz. Liz is not happy and because the problem persists, Liz wants Rachel to let Amber go. Because Amber is so committed and willing to do what it takes to improve her performance challenges, Rachel has advocated keeping Amber on and continuing to work hard together to get things right. Liz is not optimistic but has agreed—for now.

Amber, for her part, is trying to show up for work and leave without being seen. She needs her paycheck so that she can support her kids, but Amber is almost more frightened of being yelled at than she is of being fired. Amber is perpetually nervous and walks around on eggshells. She's hoping that she will do a good enough job going forward that Rachel and Liz will let her previous performance issues go. She is not looking forward to her upcoming performance review and is trying to figure out how to call in sick.

> *The quality of our lives depends not on whether or not we have conflicts, but on how we respond to them.* – Tom Crum, as quoted in Leski (2013)

What is Conflict?

> *Conflict is an indicator of frustrated needs, interests, and desires.*
> – Dr. Jess Bonnan-White

Merriam-Webster's dictionary (2013) defines conflict as any difference that prevents agreement. *The Random House Dictionary* (2013) highlights struggle, controversy, discord, battle, and incompatibility. Synonyms from *Roget's Thesaurus* include clash, combat, competition, war, contention, and tug-of-war.

Psychologist Susan Heitler describes conflict as "any situation where facts, desires or fears pull or push participants against each other or in divergent directions" (Heitler, 2012, para. 2). Conflict coach Cinnie Noble describes the cost of conflict to organizations as "[l]ow morale and productivity, stress, illness, absenteeism, [and] litigation due to unnecessary disputes" (Noble, 2003).

No matter how we define or describe conflict, everyone knows what it is, what it feels like, and how we'd rather avoid it, if at all possible. We do not want our needs, interests, or desires to be frustrated in any way, whether this frustration comes from a rub by others or from our own internal misalignment.

What's Good About Conflict?

In their book, *Interpersonal Conflict, 5th Edition*, William W. Wilmot and Joyce L. Hocker (1998) identify some key benefits to conflict. These include:

- Raising awareness that a problem exists;
- Challenging and changing old assumptions;
- Discussing conflict and working together, which means coming up with better solutions more quickly; and
- Creating opportunities for people to mature, develop, build skills, and to highlight what is most important to them, the relationship, and the organization (if applicable).

Without conflict—a "rub" between what is and what could be—problems can fester. These are not little problems, but problems that are holding back the maturity, effectiveness, and functioning of individuals and organizations. Ongoing, unaddressed conflict also limits the strength and health of relationships between individuals and between an individual and her/his own self-image.

Disclosure: I'm a Conflict Cheerleader!

No, I do not like to stir up conflict, nor do I enjoy conflict. Trust me on that one! I do, however, like to look at the bright side of conflict and how things can grow and get better as a result of conflicts that are bound to occur.

I am a trained and certified mediator. By the time this book is released, I expect to be volunteering again as a community mediator and to have begun providing conflict resolution coaching services to local nonprofits and churches.

I admit—I LOVE mediation! A basic principle of mediation is that I, as the mediator, do not resolve any conflicts. Instead, I help people to have the conversations they need to have and develop the plans they need to develop in order to resolve their own conflicts in their own way.

I also provide examples of (and teach people) how to be more successful in mediating their own conflicts. Certainly, the conflict that brings people to mediation is not their first conflict, nor is it likely to be their last. Participating in a healthy and effective process that includes negotiating, validating, supporting, confronting, and agreeing with those whom you may have characterized as enemies means that you are likely to use these tools in the future. By becoming more adept at problem solving and conflict resolution, people are less likely to have to resort to legal resources. It builds your confidence and your ability to resolve your own conflicts quickly in a way that honors your own desires, as well as those of others.

My approach to mediation and to conflict coaching is much different than you may have seen characterized on television or experienced by yourself directly. Many mediators are attorneys. People often approach attorneys for mediation help if their conflict (or "case") is legally actionable.

What most people don't realize (and frankly, don't care about in the heat of the moment) is that lawyers have a win-lose orientation in terms of their education and professional goals. There is nothing wrong with that, if you are trying to win a court case. Mediation, however, has a different orientation. It is designed to help people resolve their own conflicts. With my background in the social work field (over twenty years of experience—part of my "E" in GOD ASSETS), I understand cooperative problem solving in a way that is different from that of most attorneys. It is not a matter of right or wrong; it is simply a different orientation.

I learned in mediation training (and saw frequently in practice) that attorneys tend to have a high "D" personality or temperament (their T in GOD ASSETS). They have a strong desire to dominate and be in charge. They also tend to be very competitive. It is hard for them not to call a right or wrong or a good or bad in mediation negotiations. They automatically lean toward arbitration, where they make the decision on who is right and who is wrong in a given situation.

As a mediation student, I noticed that it was extremely difficult for the attorneys in my class to stay patient and spend the time to allow both sides to get their issues off their chests verbally (a process that could take hours). If you need an advocate in the courtroom, that's who you want. If you need someone to support YOU as being in charge, that's another matter altogether.

I emphasize this because most people enter and remain in conflict by acting a lot like lawyers: "I'm right, you're wrong; I win, you lose." In healthy, effective conflict and resolution, this approach will not work.

> *There is little value in preparing a cookbook of recipes for conflict success. The effects of conflict interaction depend directly on what the participants do mentally with conflict behaviors—that is, how they process and interpret those behaviors.* – William Cupach and Daniel Canary, as quoted in Leski (2013)

The mental interpretation of what's happening during a conflict, how people behave, and what people are willing to do to resolve the conflict is part of how God made each of us. It is also dependent on the conflict: where it is, with whom, and what the stakes are in terms of outcome.

Conflict Style Inventories

Conflict Style Inventories are assessment tools that identify ways that people tend most often to respond to conflict. These are assessments in the same way that we assess our personality or temperament, our spiritual gifts, our values, and our strengths.

There are a lot of theories concerning conflict and conflict management, and various popular conflict style inventories. One such inventory is the Thomas Kilmann Conflict Mode Instrument (TKI).

Thomas Kilmann Conflict Mode Instrument

The Thomas Kilmann Conflict Mode Instrument (TKI) identifies five conflict-handling modes, methods of conflict resolution that have been identified from studying 59,000 people in the U.S. and 6,000 people from sixteen other countries (Kilmann Diagnostics, n.d.).

Of these five modes, each is rated on two dimensions:

- **Assertiveness**, or how much a person in conflict wishes to satisfy her/his own interests and concerns; and
- **Cooperativeness**, or the extent to which a person in conflict goes to satisfy the concerns and interests of the other party or parties.

Each of the modes is perceived to be "good" or "right" in certain situations; therefore, no approach is uniformly better than the others.

Everyone is perceived as being able to use all five modes. Based on an individual's temperament, the situation, their experiences, and other factors, people may tend to rely more heavily on one or two approaches than the others.

The report you get from the assessment will tell you how often you use that particular mode of problem solving in comparison to the study sample and when each mode is best used in a conflict. People taking the assessment will also receive some coaching questions to ask themselves regarding their use of each of the modes, depending upon how often they use each of them.

The TKI modes are as follows:

- **Competing** is power-oriented, using whatever power sources are available to secure the person's own interests in the conflict. Competing is assertive and uncooperative.
- **Accommodating** is the opposite of competing. It is self-sacrificing, putting the other person's concerns and interests above one's own. Accommodation is unassertive and cooperative.
- **Avoiding** occurs when a person refuses or declines to address the conflict at all. Avoidance is unassertive and uncooperative because the person does not directly pursue their own interests or the interests of others.

- **Collaborating** is the opposite of avoiding. Collaboration means pursuing a resolution that is acceptable to both parties. It is both assertive and cooperative.
- **Compromising** is an effort to find a fast solution that partially satisfies the interests and needs of both parties. Unlike collaborating, compromising means putting in less effort to understand and to be understood. It is moderate in both assertiveness and cooperativeness.

(Consulting Psychologists Press, 2001)

Each of the TKI modes is connected to one of the four temperament types and to type indicators in the Myers-Briggs Personality Inventory. We discuss temperament more in chapter 9.

The Word on Conflict

As an asset, God uses our different conflict styles to teach each other how to resolve disagreements and stalemate positions among Christians. Each style has a purpose and a time to be used to build unity and to provide solutions in any organization and community.

Certainly, there is biblical support for each of the ways that conflict can be handled in this theory. For example:

- **Competing** can be supported by Proverbs 24:5: Answer a fool in simple terms so he doesn't get a swelled head (MSG).
- **Accommodating** can be supported by Romans 12:10: Love each other as brothers and sisters, and honor others more than you do yourself (CEV).
- **Avoiding** can be supported by Proverbs 24:4: Don't answer the foolish arguments of fools, or you will become as foolish as they are (NLT).
- **Collaborating** can be supported by Philippians 2:4: Let each of you look not only to his own interests, but also to the interests of others (ESV).

- **Compromising** can be supported by Romans 12:18: Do all that you can to live in peace with everyone (NLT).

Since the Bible does support various ways to resolve conflict, we can be sure that God has provided among His people different strengths in the different methods for resolving conflict. This propensity or level of comfort is part of God's unique design for you.

It is essential to:

- Prayerfully prepare to address conflict
- Be aware of signs of conflict
- Be willing to address conflict directly to resolve it
- Know the various conflict styles—the ones you prefer, and the ones you may need more help implementing
- Enlist the help of a mentor to directly and effectively address issues
- Take a biblical approach to conflict resolution
- Pursue peace (Psalm 34:14; Hebrews 12:14)
- Understand that resolution of the most difficult conflicts may not be possible by our efforts alone (Romans 12:18)
- Anticipate positive change, however it comes

Conflict is a part of life. Although it is difficult, do not let it overwhelm you. Learn and grow from it whenever possible, and share the benefits of this process with others.

Coaching Questions

If your GOD ASSETS were the recipe to your favorite dish, what ingredient might your conflict style be? Why is that so?

Consider the Thomas-Kilmann conflict model.

- Which of these approaches and/or scriptures resonates most with you? Do you have a sense that some conflict styles are "better" than others?

The GOD ASSETS: God's Investment in You and What to Do With It

- What are some other factors that influence the conflict style we choose to use to approach an issue?

> *Conflict is an opportunity for change and peace-building.* – Dr. Jess Bonnan-White

Consider an area of conflict you may be experiencing now, or one you have experienced recently.

- Identify one area in which the conflict has, or is, providing you an opportunity to change.
- Identify a new peace-building skill you are learning as a result of this conflict.

> *All conflict management styles have their place. Someone who is able to shift to each style as called for is probably going to be the most successful at dealing with conflict, as well as the happiest person in the long run.* – Alden Swan, co-author of *The Gospel Uncensored* and blogger on mediation and conflict resolution.

Consider again the area of conflict you are experiencing now, or one you have experienced recently.

- Which of the conflict styles have you been using to resolve the conflict?
- If this style is not effective, to which style do you need to change?
- What is one thing you can do soon in order to make that necessary shift?
- How might this happen?

Chapter 7
Style of Leadership

Both Liz and her father, William, are experiencing versions of an attempted leadership takeover at their respective companies.

William's approach to leadership is participatory and cautious. He has led this way since he started at the organization. William has consistently been promoted and now serves as the CEO of his Fortune 500 company. His leadership style has apparently worked well for the organization so far.

John, as senior vice-president, doesn't see it that way. John constantly challenges William's leadership decisions and style. John is the grandson of the company's founder and is two decades younger than William. John believes that William's leadership style is not "definitive" or "authoritative" enough. John has some definite ideas about the way things should be done, and he wants them done his way—right now. John believes that the company can go farther with a different leadership style at the helm: his own.

Liz is also facing a constant challenge from someone who reports to her. Liz is the founder and CEO of her own nonprofit organization. Her chief financial officer (CFO), Chris, is not much older than Liz.

However, he sees himself as more "seasoned" and "experienced" than Liz in a variety of matters.

Chris goes beyond overseeing the financial operations of the organization and takes liberties in providing unsolicited evaluations of how Liz handles matters of personnel, publicity, and community relations. He has even suggested the best office schedule for Liz to keep! Chris's approach is one of feigned concern over the well-being of the organization. His true agenda is unclear, but his lack of genuine feeling is abundantly clear to anyone observing. To make matters worse, Chris's performance as CFO is less than outstanding.

Will and Liz have each realized on their own that their leadership styles have set the standard for how people approach them, what boundaries people are allowed to cross, and the outcomes of each person's job performance. They have talked over dinner several times about ways that they address conflict and the styles of leadership that may be best used in their respective organizations.

What is a Leader?

Leadership is a role that we fulfill (Williams, 1989). If you have a desire and responsibility to help others "be all that they can be" in work, service, personal development, or spiritual growth, then you are a leader. If you want to succeed on your own and to serve as an example to other people, then you are a leader. That includes everyone!

Certainly, people with specific titles and roles in organizations serve as leaders. Whether these people are good leaders or bad ones, strong leaders or weak ones, effective or ineffective leaders, they are still leaders. For example, parents are leaders in their families by virtue of their age, responsibilities, and their titles. Teachers in school and supervisors at work also fall under the definition of leaders, since their responsibilities include helping students and employees develop skills for success, improve performance, and consistently deliver high-quality work.

Most people lead by example, without an official title. For example, a sports figure may be a leader because she inspires others to work diligently toward their goals. She may not be an official coach or team captain, but she serves a leadership function by offering a good example to other players in her sport, in other sports, and to those outside the world of sports who want to succeed.

Each of these types of leadership (role and function) is invaluable, and each is an ASSET that God gives us.

Leaders are Made, Not Born

The phrase "natural-born leader" refers to a set of temperament traits and natural strengths that meld together well with a particularly well-honed leadership style. One of these components is innate, another is developed only by experience, and the third is a combination of the two. Because some key components of leadership can only be developed by experience, *all leaders are made.*

While some leaders are born into their titles and positions (think royalty) and therefore provide a leadership role, no one is born into the components of leadership that go beyond that. Think about teachers or principals you've had, supervisors at work, or even pastors at church. Were they all natural-born leaders, or were some leaders by default in their role?

Just as we develop into spouses, parents, or our roles in the workplace over time, we also develop into leaders over time. Each of us can cultivate strong leadership skills.

The notion that some people are born to lead while others have to work at it is based on the assumption that there is largely one type of leader: dynamic, outspoken, opinionated, negotiating, charming, etc. As we will learn, there are many types of leaders, which means that each of us can fulfill a leadership role in our own style at any time.

Developing as a Role Leader

Williams (1989) identifies four stages of Christian leadership development:

- **Anointing** – Identification by God that you have been assigned or gifted to serve in a particular leadership role or office. This identification comes long before we are released to actually serve in the area of anointing. For example, David was anointed king years before he served in that office.
- **Preparation** – Praying, discerning, studying, and learning are key to serving successfully in leadership roles. 2 Timothy 2:15 tells us that studying will be a demonstration that God has approved us for the roles in which we are serving, and will help us to be confident when we are released to serve in our specific roles.
- **Practice** – It is apparent to me that many people are driving around my town who have not had sufficient driving practice! I also remember a time when I led a song as a guest worshiper at a church, and I had not practiced. What a disaster that was! Practice makes perfect, so before we are appointed for official roles, we should have had some hands-on practice in our service capacity. The more practice we have, the more likely we are to be confident and competent in our role.
- **Appointing** – At this point, it is official! God has called us; we are prepared intellectually, spiritually, and practically; and we are ready to serve as leaders in both role and function.

Leadership Styles

There are many different leadership style frameworks. One of the most detailed is the framework from Bill Hybels, founder and senior pastor of Willow Creek Community Church in South Barrington, Illinois. Hybels (2002) offers ten examples of leadership styles:

1. **Visionary** – These are powerful vision-casters who are passionate, idealistic, and faith-filled.
2. **Directional** – These wise leaders have a God-given ability to choose the right direction for an organization, particularly in times of change.
3. **Strategic** – These leaders take a vision and turn it into a step-by-step plan of action.
4. **Managing** – These are organized leaders who pull together people, resources, and processes to achieve a goal, mission, or objective. This leadership style ensures that things get done.
5. **Motivational** – This is an interpersonal leader who inspires and encourages his/her team members through relationship building toward the vision or goal.
6. **Shepherding** – Like motivational leaders, shepherding leaders inspire via relationship building, but their focus is on building a strong community where people can be nurtured.
7. **Team-Building** – Focusing on right results, team-builders have the unique ability to identify a group of people with the proper balance of personality, ability, chemistry, etc., each in his or her proper role on the team.
8. **Entrepreneurial** – Armed with any other leadership style, entrepreneurial leaders function best when they are implementing a new idea or vision. Otherwise, they lose confidence, focus, or interest.
9. **Re-engineering** – Taking a troubled organization or situation and turning it around is how reengineering leaders excel and thrive.

10. **Bridge-Building** – Gifted diplomats and negotiators with patience, flexibility, and the willingness to compromise, bridge-building leaders have the ability to bring a wide range of constituent groups under one umbrella organization.

Good leaders will use different styles and approaches to leadership based on the circumstances, goals, and needs of those they are leading. Most of us, however, "default" to those leadership styles with which we are most comfortable, whether or not these styles are most effective.

Leadership Effectiveness

Bill Hybels describes leadership effectiveness this way: "I am increasingly convinced that highly effective leaders often have impact not only because they are highly gifted, but also because their leadership styles mesh perfectly with specific ministry needs" (Hybels, 2002, p. 141).

There is no one, single, effective style of leadership. Every organization, situation, relationship, or role not only calls for a different style of leadership based on a variety of factors, but different leadership styles may be required simultaneously.

As an asset, leadership provides direction. These include standards and guidelines and ways of doing and being that others can emulate. Leaders are an asset because they bring out the best in those they lead, and their skills are a blessing to all.

Because the leadership needs in the body of Christ are great, God has not only provided the body with individuals who have the spiritual gift of leadership, but He has also equipped them with different leadership styles. God has also given all individuals the ability to serve as leaders in various capacities—again, whether they hold a position, title, or role officially or not.

Leadership Pitfalls and Dysfunctions: Leadership's Dark Side

People step into leadership roles and behavior based on a variety of factors. A calling from the Lord to do so should be a primary factor. The need for someone to step up and take charge in any given situation in a community may be another key factor.

Personal insecurities and failures that we have experienced in the past often compel us to become leaders. People who are insecure, who feel inferior and/or are looking for approval from others, often become phenomenally successful leaders (McIntosh & Rima, 2007).

Equally as often, the same insecurities that serve as success motivators can also be the downfall of men and women with powerful, God-given leadership potential. It is important to be aware of this and watch out for it as you work as a role or functional leader.

Christian communities (churches, organizations, groups, businesses, etc.) have to be particularly aware of potential leadership pitfalls (McIntosh & Rima, 2007). Because ambition, control, and power plays are sometimes disguised in Christian language (such as headship and obedience), dysfunctions in leaders and in leadership arrangements often go undetected for extended periods of time—sometimes until it is too late to repair the damage.

McIntosh & Rima (2007) describe the dark side of leadership—the compulsions, urges, or "fleshly" aspects of our personalities that can both drive us to success as leaders and that remain unknown to us until they create catastrophic problems. This "darkness" casts a shadow on what we are working to accomplish and the process we use to go about it.

Primary shadows include:

- Pride (Proverbs 11:2; Proverbs 29:23)
- Selfishness (Romans 2:8; James 3:14, 16)
- Self-Deception and Wrong Motives (Jeremiah 17:9; 1 Corinthians 4:3-4)

The same way that there are leadership styles, there are also leadership dysfunction styles:

- **Compulsive** leaders must maintain absolute order. They are prone to occasional public outbursts of anger, are perfectionists, are keenly status-conscious, are overly moralistic and judgmental, and are frequently critical of others. Marriages, churches, and lives have been broken (some irreparably) as a result of this type of leadership.
- **Narcissistic** leaders are centered on themselves. They have an inflated sense of self-importance, exhibit a constant need for attention from others, overemphasize their achievements and contributions, and lack empathy. They often use the organizations or groups that they lead as personal platforms to launch themselves in their careers. This type of leadership can result in the exploitation of people, and the destruction of churches and other organizations for the sole purpose of feeding the ego of the leader.
- **Paranoid** leaders have a constant fear that someone or something will undermine their authority. They are jealous of the gifts of others and perpetually concerned about rebellion. These leaders limit the authority of their subordinates and are extremely sensitive to the mildest form of criticism. Distrust at minimum, and factions, enemies, and warfare at the maximum, can result from the actions of paranoid leaders.
- **Co-dependent** leaders strive to please others. It is difficult for them to say no or to disappoint other people, and they

avoid confrontation. They often take personal responsibility for things outside their control, including the behaviors of others. These leaders are most likely to destroy themselves, their careers, their health, their marriages, and their finances trying to please others.
- **Passive-Aggressive** leaders will delay, deny, resist, and become otherwise inefficient in order to avoid performing tasks that they find undesirable. They may frequently complain and harbor bitterness, creating a demoralizing environment for their team. Measurements and systems of control are often resisted. These leaders live with the shame of their own behavior, as their leadership roles are often unstable and short-lived.

Steps to overcoming these challenges include:

1. Acknowledging that the "dark side" exists and believing that the Holy Spirit will help you to overcome this challenge;
2. Examining your past, the events that have shaped your life, and the feelings associated with these;
3. Resisting the placement of unrealistic expectations on yourself or others;
4. Using spiritual disciplines such as journaling, retreats, and accountability to help you see yourself in the mirror of Scripture; and
5. Understanding your value in Christ and having faith that your value and worth truly come from Him.

Dr. Sarah Sumner (2006) offers an experience-based framework for defining leadership and the character issues that can propel or impede progress in this area. Her "People Model" of leadership describes three types of leaders based on Plato's philosophical ideals: True, Good, and Beautiful.

- **Strategists (True)** tend to shed light on problems in order to identify the truth and to face challenges head on. Their goal is to make their organizations more authentic and to have the people who are part of the organization experience freedom from the burdens of unidentified problems. Strategists bring accountability, order, and clarity to their organizations, with a focus on integrity. The communication style of strategists is very straightforward: they concentrate on the content of what is said rather than on how it is said, which leads people to often perceive them as confrontational. They want their organizations to BE good.
- **Humanitarians (Good)** want to bring compassion to the workplace by making it a comfortable place to work. They desire to nurture their employees so that they don't lose their commitment, creativity, and drive. These leaders see integrity and unity as similar concepts and see members of their organization as a family. Humanitarians want their organizations to FEEL good, and they concentrate in their communication style on how things are said. They are perceived as tolerant and patient.
- **Diplomats (Beautiful)** believe that it is important to project a positive image for their organization. They desire to create a sense of internal peace in the workings of the company by being tactful and by avoiding or quickly resolving conflicts with external stakeholders. Diplomatic leaders want their organizations to LOOK good. In communication, they always look for the right time to say what they need to say and are perceived as non-confrontational.

While each leadership style has definite strengths, there are some significant areas of weakness for each as well. When leaders engage in these weaker or negative areas, they are leading "below the line."

- In their effort to focus on the issue at hand and resolve it, Strategists (True) can neglect others and their feelings,

contributions, or opinions to some degree. They can become self-righteous, asserting that their thoughts and ways are the only ones that are correct and that they are the only ones in the organization who care about integrity. They can be presumptuous about the motivations and commitments of others and be impatient for change.
- In their effort to make everyone comfortable, Humanitarians (Good) can become self-serving fairly quickly. They, too, want to be comfortable in their environments, and their actions can reflect self-interests. Because they fear not being liked by others, they tend to enable the negative, destructive behavior of other team members.
- In their focus on image, Diplomats (Beautiful) can become self-centered and self-absorbed, almost narcissistic in their effort to maintain a good image for themselves. They tend to distort truth for the sake of their image.

Functioning while motivated by pride, fear, or deceitfulness all cause individuals, families, groups, and organizations to be ineffective and unhealthy. So how might these problems of leadership be fixed?

- **Humility:** Strategists often suffer from pride, so they need more humility in dealing with others. A strategist's ways are not the only way to resolve problems, or even the best way. Becoming more humble will bring self-awareness and improve the quality of relationships with others.
- **Courage:** Humanitarians suffer from fear of hurting or alienating others, so they need more courage. They need to believe that addressing issues honestly does not mean that they are being unkind, disloyal, or unsupportive. Courage to speak up and pursue resolutions will actually help Humanitarians create more of the environment that they desire.

- **Honesty:** Diplomats want a sense of perfection in their organizations: structure, balance, and civility. They need to understand that covering problems up does not make them go away, and that challenges will continue to emerge unless rectified. They need to be more honest about the problems in their organizations and be willing to address these in a way that continues to develop the type of organization they desire.

Leadership in Our Recipe

I spent a lot of time and space on leadership styles, strengths, and weaknesses in order to share a picture with you of how this works "on the ground," in the reality of our lives.

Understanding how we lead naturally, when we are leading by example (function) versus role (title), what leadership tools and styles there are, which leadership styles work best for us in which situations, and how the pitfalls of leadership can derail God's best plan for us—all of this knowledge and behavior helps to provide some parameters of the recipe of God in us.

In our GOD ASSETS recipe, effective leadership is an activator. In recipes, activator ingredients get the other ingredients cooking! They draw heat and break down the other ingredients more quickly for their specific purposes. Like a recipe activator, leadership helps us to build upon the other ingredients in our unique God-given recipe.

Specifically, leadership helps us to:

1. Exercise our *faith* in areas outside of our own needs and priorities;
2. Communicate our *values* to others through action and planning;
3. Reflect a genuine, passionate *drive and devotion* to a group of people and/or a cause;

4. Maximize use of our natural *abilities* and talents;
5. Practice resolving *conflicts* between ourselves and others and between our team members, using various conflict resolution styles;
6. Integrate what we have learned from past *experiences* into the task, team, job, or service we are providing now;
7. Demonstrate how we regulate the negative effects of our *temperament*; and
8. Use our spiritual *gifts* properly.

Coaching Questions

- What are the top three ways in which I am serving as a functional (by example) leader?
- What are the top three ways in which I have functioned as a role (by title and/or responsibility) leader?
- What positive leadership traits do I consistently exhibit?
- What is one negative leadership trait of mine that I want to improve quickly?
- How am I using my other "recipe ingredients" in my GOD ASSETS to help me be a better leader?
- How are my strong leadership skills helping me to activate my GOD ASSETS in other areas of my life?
- If my GOD ASSETS are not activated, how can I use my leadership skills and experiences to help me do so?
- What are my next steps?

The GOD ASSETS: God's Investment in You and What to Do With It

Chapter 8

Experiences

Liz has the opportunity to exercise many new leadership skills in a conflict between staff at her nonprofit organization.

Rachel is a supervisor at Liz's nonprofit. She is highly skilled and very efficient at what she does. She was promoted quickly because of the high quality of work she delivers and because of her consistency and reliability. Rachel comes from a strong, middle-class family, and she graduated with honors from a prestigious state university. She was always a distinguished student—honor roll, extracurricular activities, volunteer work, and high citizenship. These successes have followed Rachel throughout her career as well. She expects the best because that has been her experience, and she expects the best from her team members.

Amber, whom we met in chapter 2, is more laid back than Rachel would like. Amber comes from a family of modest means that moved around a lot for work. She has an associate's degree, but that was hard-earned between holding down two jobs, a marriage, and babies. Amber's attachments to friends or professional colleagues are limited; she largely keeps to herself. Amber is more likely to wait for a specific instruction or directive than she is to take initiative to resolve a problem. As someone who is rarely in charge, taking the lead and being innovative does not come naturally to her. According to Rachel, nothing beyond her children seems to elicit enthusiasm from Amber.

The quality of work that Amber delivers is not up to the standards that Rachel has set for her department. Rachel has been in talks with Liz about disciplinary action and possible termination of Amber.

Liz can relate to both Amber and Rachel. Like Rachel, Liz is a real go-getter and is highly successful. Like Amber, Liz has been a single mom to two children, and she understands how difficult it can be to balance family and work. While she can relate to Amber, Liz can only imagine what life is really like for her. Amber's income is much lower than Liz's; Amber's children are younger than Liz's; and, from what Liz can gather, Amber does not have the level of emotional, financial, and tangible family support that Liz enjoys.

Rachel, who is single, cannot relate to Amber's "issues." Amber, who is struggling, cannot relate to Liz or to Rachel, both whom seem to have it all together and to operate with ease at all times. Liz empathizes with Amber, but agrees with Rachel: success toward the mission is bigger than the problems of any individual employee.

Each woman has her own vantage point, particularly because each has her own set of experiences.

Which of these women can you relate to most so far, and why?

Experience: An Essential Recipe Ingredient

Experience is the ingredient that God can always use immediately for His purposes. It is much like the flour in a cake recipe. Flour provides gluten, which gets a bad rap lately. However, gluten is a protein, which is a nutritional building block. Flour also gives the cake shape and form. As important as this flour is in the recipe, it only works when it is combined with other ingredients and it is agitated (i.e., shaken or stirred up). If you over-mix the flour with other ingredients, it makes your cake tough (Horn, 2013). Who wants a "tough cookie" when you can have a nice, warm, moist slice of cake?

Experiential and Developmental Assets: It's What's Inside and Outside That Counts

The Search Institute in Minneapolis has identified forty developmental assets for children and youth. (The link in the references for this chapter provides a list of all forty developmental assets and their respective categories.) These assets are milestones and experiences that young people should have in order to help them to develop into "healthy, caring and responsible" adults.

These experiences help to shape key parts of who those children will grow up to be and how they will grow up to serve. Childrens' positive, negative, or lack of experiences in these areas are all assets that God can use to help them in their ministries, careers, and contributions to the world.

A child of divorce, Geoffrey Canada grew up in the Bronx, New York. Geoffrey's father left his family and did not provide financial or emotional support to the children. Geoffrey's neighborhood environment was one that plagues many large cities: poverty, crime, violence, drugs, truancy, abandoned homes, and strife.

The list of Developmental Assets has two categories. External Assets are resources that a child has from outside of herself, or strengths that child needs to succeed in his environment. Internal Assets include intrinsic motivations, skills, values. and attitudes—resources from within.

Geoffrey lacked many of the ***External Assets*** or resources that would support him in growing up to be a contributing citizen. A caring neighborhood (#4 on the list of External Developmental Assets), caring school environment (#5), and safety (#10) are three assets from the list that we can quickly identify that Geoffrey lacked growing up.

As a child, Geoffrey's mother was very committed to education and created an environment of educational and developmental support for Geoffrey and his three brothers. From the list of Developmental Assets, Mrs. Canada developed a relationship with her sons and helped to cultivate within them many of the ***Internal Assets*** on the list through teaching and example: achievement motivation (#21), responsibility (#30), resistance skills (#35), and a positive view of their personal future (#40). These assets helped to mitigate some of the lack of positive external assets described previously. Geoffrey's mother and her support system also provided many of the ***External Assets***: family support (#1), positive family communication (#2), family boundaries (#11), and adult role models (#14). These helped to mitigate some of the possible negative effects of resource or asset shortcomings.

So, did Geoffrey turn to a life of crime or mediocrity because of his lack of assets growing up? Not at all! Geoffrey turned the combination of these negative experiences and his positive family environment into assets for himself and for those he now serves.

As a result of his lack of external assets, Geoffrey developed a drive and devotion to education and to disadvantaged youth. He says he understood his life purpose and calling at an early age. He made a quick and early commitment to education. He has earned bachelor's and master's degrees *and* has received honorary doctoral degrees from several institutions.

Mr. Canada is now a nationally known and respected education reformer. He is CEO and founder of the Harlem Children's Zone (HCZ). Geoffrey Canada has been described as articulate, smart, innovative, passionate, charismatic, and even a "superman." Mr. Canada is a Heinz Award recipient and was listed as one of *Time Magazine's* 100 most influential people in the world in 2011.

He was centrally featured in the 2010 documentary, *Waiting for Superman*. President Barack Obama's Promise Neighborhoods initiative was modeled after Canada's Harlem Children's Zone.

How Experience Shapes Our Role

As we can see, Mr. Canada's experiences—positive, painful, and negative—all helped to shape and form who God intended him to be and how God intended him to serve. Part of what has given Mr. Canada such a broad, worldwide stage to discuss educational reform is his negative experiences with his own education and environment growing up. He can relate closely to the experiences of the children at the HCZ, and he is able to see positive assets where many would possibly only see the negative.

The Mask

Oftentimes, we believe that only our positive experiences are worth being used by God to help others or to fulfill a calling. How can we help others in an area in which we have failed or where we have had nothing but poor experiences?

Often, in order to serve in the area of our passion (our drive, desire, devotion, and dedication that we discussed in chapter 5), we "hide" our failures and put on a mask of our successes. Sometimes, the mask we put on is even manufactured from successes that we have not yet experienced.

Suppose you were a D+ student in school. You had minimal family support, and your neighborhood was a rough place in which to grow up. You did not attend college, or you did not finish. You now have children, and you're a role model to your nieces and nephews. You want them to get a good education, but your story is one of success without one.

The GOD ASSETS: God's Investment in You and What to Do With It

What do you do? Do you say, "Hey, you don't need a degree or good grades! Just hope for the best when you get older!" No, of course not. Instead, you may share some of your struggles, but you give them the "do-as-I-say-not-as-I-did" speech. You point them in the direction of examples of people (like Mr. Canada) who have an education and are doing meaningful work.

There is nothing wrong with that, but remember: you would not have such a clear vantage point from which to instruct, direct, encourage, and pray for those kids in your environment if you had not had the experiences you had in the past.

Tell them how hard it was for you growing up and how hard it has been for you as an adult without an education. Tell them what your hopes are for them and what aspects of your own educational or professional life you want them to avoid.

Your experience can be a great teacher.

Experience: The Great Teacher

There are many examples of how both successes and failures are great teachers.

It's great to get marriage advice from people who have been happily married for decades. We can just follow their steps and try to get there. But one thing they have is *blind spots*. Their consistent success has blocked them from gaining knowledge and direct experience of particular types of marital struggles. That's great for them, but what if your marriage is in trouble? How will you get encouragement or develop a skill to help strengthen it? A couple that has successfully overcome marriage struggles and trials may be a better resource for that support.

We often go for career advice to people who are in positions that we want. We ask questions like: How did you become CEO/

director/manager/VP/chief? How did you enter your field and succeed? If you have been successful in your career, one thing is for sure: you have many stories of failures along the way. How many positions did you apply for and not get? How many times did you submit a proposal that did not get accepted? How many times did you set a goal in your position and fail to reach it? Has "re-engineering" or "downsizing" affected your position? What stories and experiences would you share with someone who is new in the field?

"What is that you have in your hand?"

God picked Moses to help him meet the needs of His people. God saw His people as being afflicted, crying, and oppressed. He related to their sufferings, sorrows, and trials. The Lord decided to intervene on their behalf and told Moses that he was being sent to have a conversation with the master oppressor—Pharaoh (Exodus 3:1-10).

Moses, being like most of the rest of us, first reacted with what can only be called, at the least, apprehension! Moses gave a response akin to, "Who, me?" God said, "Yes, you! And I'm going with you. Your success will be a sign that I sent you" (from Exodus 3:11-12).

Moses then started fretting about the details. His mind was on what kind of authority he would be able to show when he rolled up to Pharaoh and demanded some liberties that the people had never seen. God told him in detail what to say and how to say it. He told Moses how to speak to Pharaoh, to the people of Israel, and to the rulers of the Israelites (Exodus 3:13-16).

God again told Moses that he would be successful in his endeavor, and that the people would benefit greatly. God even gave Moses details—things to look for along the way to indicate that he was moving toward reaching his goal (Exodus 3:17-22).

The GOD ASSETS: God's Investment in You and What to Do With It

But again, like most of us, Moses did not see himself as having authority (Exodus 4:1). Moses was not *intentionally* denying the power of God. Moses was just not confident that others would acknowledge God's power if it was working through him personally.

How many times have we felt that way? We have a message burning in our hearts from the Lord, but we don't share it because we don't think people will receive the message from us. Perhaps we feel we don't have the authority because we don't have a certain position or title and that God should send someone else. Maybe we lack education or certification in an area of expertise. Maybe we've had a huge public fall such as a failed marriage, repeating a grade in school, a job termination, addiction, prosecution and conviction, bankruptcy, a horrendous audition, or a wardrobe malfunction. We feel that people will be too busy laughing at us or rehashing our falls and failures to hear what we are saying, offering, or contributing..

God Qualifies You

There are seven billion people alive right now, so why would He pick you? The question is, *WHY NOT YOU?* We all belong to Him, so He can pick whoever He wants to get His work done. He's prepared you for such a time as this, and one of the ways He has done that is through your particular experiences.

Little do we know that God will be using our failures AND our successes to accomplish His purposes! In Exodus 4:2, when Moses protested about his abilities to complete his task and begin fulfilling his calling, God asked him, "What do you have in your hand?" Experiences are on-hand, available resources (like salt and pepper in everyone's cabinet) that can help us to relate to others and apply what we know and what we have to get God's job done. Whatever is going on, we can relate it in some way to one or more experiences we have had.

So back to Moses. What were his experiences? Moses was raised in the same household with Pharaoh. Even though he had privileges and comforts from Pharaoh's household, Moses always stood up for the Hebrew people (Exodus 2:1-10). Moses even killed an Egyptian person who was beating a Hebrew worker. When Pharaoh found out that Moses had killed an Egyptian, he tried to have Moses killed, but Moses escaped. Moses thought the deed was secret, but some Israelites reminded Moses of his error when he did step up to provide leadership (Exodus 2:11-14). By the time God approached Moses to assign him the task, Moses had already experienced a public fall and a failed leadership experience, and he was afraid of Pharaoh as a rule. He was ill-equipped, according to his own assessment.

On top of having bad experiences, Moses saw himself as being short on skills in speech. He asked for God's help and God reminded Moses that He was not short on the ability to help Moses speak. Moses, however, still asked to pass on the assignment. God gave him his request, but it was not without frustration and it wasn't a free ride. Moses still had to communicate to Aaron so Aaron could communicate to other people. Aaron would look to Moses as he would to the Lord (Exodus 4:10-16). Moses got out of speaking, but his orders were still pretty tall!

In all that, with God giving an assignment and Moses protesting about all his shortcomings, God pointed to Moses to an immediate, tangible resource. God asked Moses, "What is that in your hand?" (Exodus 4:2 AMP).

The Experience Asset as a Resource and a Reference

Of all of our GOD ASSETS, experience is the asset that is always, immediately in our hands. Only we know what we've been through, what we've accomplished, what we've seen, what we've done, what we've failed at, and where we have been a shining

The GOD ASSETS: God's Investment in You and What to Do With It

example of success. Those references can be called up at any time to help someone in need, to provide direction, to give affirmation, to relate, to serve, to share knowledge, and to shine the light of Christ in a situation.

Of course, we must be careful how we use that asset! Flour has a specific purpose, and so do experiences. For example, I am an ex-smoker. I smoked a pack or more a day of cigarettes for thirteen-and-a-half years. At this writing, I have been a nonsmoker for over thirteen-and-a-half years.

I have some experience being bound by a substance addiction: nicotine. Dependence on cigarettes is nothing less than drug addiction. It has greater withdrawal symptoms than heroin, cocaine, alcohol, marijuana, and even my beloved caffeine. Nicotine is only second to heroin on that list in terms of the increasing amount of the drug it takes over time to satisfy cravings for it (McVay, 2001). With that experience as an ex-smoker, I can relate to other people who are seeking to rid themselves of an addiction after using and abusing various substances for a time.

What I cannot relate to are some of the dangerous lifestyle practices that come with some other forms of drug dependence. For example, I know what it's like to stand out in the rain, sleet, and sub-zero temperatures to "feed my addiction," but I don't know what it's like to live in an abandoned building, to sell my belongings or my body, or to be unconscious for days because of my addiction. While my experience with nicotine can give me empathy and enable me to relate to people who need help and ministering on a personal level, misrepresenting my experience as "the same thing" as something that someone else went through would be inappropriate. It would be the opposite of how God intended the asset to be used.

Experience as Asset

How might we use our experiences as assets the way that God intended?

Empathy: Having certain experiences helps us to be able to understand the feelings and experiences of other people.

Authority: Having experience in an area (good or bad) gives us authority to teach on a topic or speak to a situation. We are experts of our own experience.

Credibility: Valid, relatable experiences not only give us authority, but make what we teach and share credible or believable to other people. People can trust what we share because we've "been there."

Testimony: We overcome by the sacrifice that Christ made for us and by sharing our experiences of the power of God in our lives with other people (Revelation 12:11). We also help others to overcome by providing encouragement and hope for them to do the same.

Example: We sometimes need a road map to follow--in our careers, to get in shape, to strengthen our relationships, to get our finances in order, etc. Having experience (both failures and successes) that demonstrate the ways we should go (or not go) are often very helpful in shortening the learning and success curve for others.

Coaching Questions

- We met Amber first in chapter 2, then throughout the book. What role might experience have in her work performance?
- What experiences (big or small) might God be encouraging you to use to help others and to fulfill your destiny?
- What is holding you back from sharing with others (in an appropriate way) how your experiences have helped to shape your successes?

The GOD ASSETS: God's Investment in You and What to Do With It

- Do you see your experiences as positive and having a purpose, even the negative ones (Genesis 50:20)? If you don't or you can't, how might you begin to move in that direction?
- What is one, single, great success in your life? How might you share it or use it as a GOD ASSET to help others?

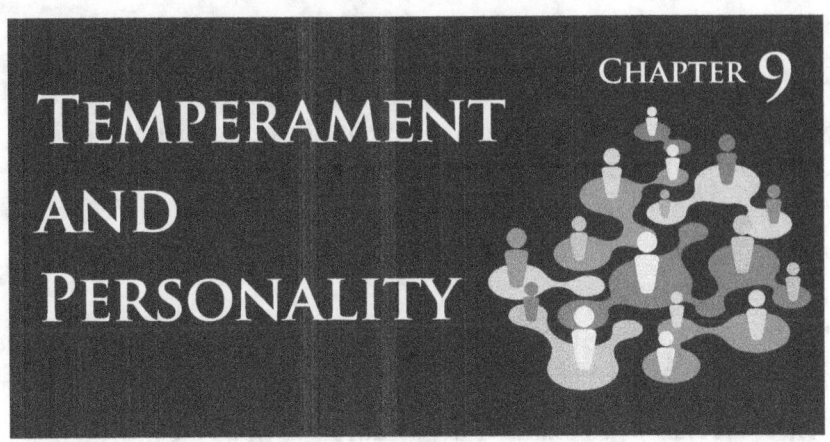

CHAPTER 9
Temperament and Personality

"I like you. Are you a sanguine?"

My family had recently moved to Central Pennsylvania, and we were joining a new church. This was our first one-on-one meeting with our new pastor. We had (finally!) finished our new members course. We were eager to be accepted as members so that we could begin serving in ministry. My new pastor was sizing me up to see how he could put me to work. He liked me, and I liked him too!

"I'm actually a choleric sanguine," I said to Pastor Cliff. "I try to keep my choleric in check early on," I joked.

"What's a sanguine?" my husband asked. He is not one for psychology or people categorizing.

My pastor jumped right in to explain. "A sanguine is someone who is popular, likable..." and some other stuff I don't remember, but his description was dead on.

"Whose face comes to mind with that description?" I asked my husband. He and I knew a thoroughbred sanguine in common.

Without hesitation, he answered, "Uh, your sister." Bingo.

Bingo! Your Temperament Fits You to a "T"

You are someone's "bingo" too! God designed you that way in His amazing recipe. There is a temperament description with your name on it. Everyone who knows you well can describe which of the well-known temperament types or personality categories you fit into best. Better yet, they can describe the category that fits into the uniqueness of YOU.

The Four Temperaments

There are many personality categorizations, but all are based on the classic, basic four temperaments or humors. Throughout history, the four temperaments have been categorized according to medical models, psychology, physiology, metaphysics, and philosophy. It was originally believed that an individual's behavior and personality could be affected by an imbalance of four different types of fluids in the body. Each of these fluids was believed to represent one of the elements: earth, wind, fire, and air. (Try not to flash back to music from the 1970s and 80s right now!)

Over the centuries, most of the fluid/element theories were discredited. However, much work had been built upon some understanding of these categories, so the categories themselves stuck. From there, the four basic (psychological, personality) temperaments were developed. Almost all personality theory and assessments currently in use (Myers-Briggs, True Colors, Enneagram, Keirsey Temperament Sorter, DiSC Assessment, Kilmann Conflict Modes, Pavlov, Adler, Fromm, etc.) have roots in the idea of the four basic temperaments or personality styles (Two-Factor Models of Personality, 2013).

Overview of the Four Temperaments

The *star* of the four temperaments is the **sanguine**. Sanguines are the life of every party. They love to be seen and love to be the center of attention. They are emotionally and physically expressive. Sanguines are likely to be upbeat and bubbly and will touch people when they speak with them. Whether it is a ministry task, a work assignment, or a home responsibility, sanguines want to make it fun. They are creative, highly energetic, and enthusiastic. They have a flair for the colorful and dramatic.

Sanguines are known for their "bursts." They are high energy! They talk a lot to whomever it is convenient. They may become angry quickly or demonstrate other emotional outbursts. These dissipate fairly quickly, and the sanguine will likely return to his or her normal, bubbly self. They are prone to disorganization and messiness. To get things in order, they may exert a short "burst" of energy or time to do what it takes to get through the next tasks, assignment, or expectation. Don't be startled if a sanguine grabs you and hugs you without warning.

The *boss* of the four temperaments is the **choleric**. If you want something done, grab a choleric! Cholerics are active, busy, independent, confident, organized, and productive. Generally, they are extroverts; however, they are also prone to working independently. They are extremely goal-oriented, are quick to make decisions, and find themselves in charge of everything. Cholerics are quick to make decisions and are excellent in emergency situations.

Cholerics are natural motivators and are careful to speak up only when they are certain that the answer they are offering is correct. They are often not popular because of their bossy natures and over-confidence, and they're okay with that. Cholerics are goal-setters and are not discouraged by adversity or challenges. In fact, they thrive on competition or opposition.

The *brains* of the four temperaments is the **melancholic**. Aristotle is quoted as having said of melancholics that, "All men of genius are of melancholic temperament," or, "*Melancholy* men, of all others, are the most witty." Melancholics are very analytical, deep thinkers. They do not take information at face value: they want to know more. Melancholics have extremely high standards for themselves and for others. They are serious and purposeful in their approach to any task. Melancholics are perfectionists and believe that anything worth doing is worth doing well, properly, and as close to perfectly as possible.

Of all the temperament types, the melancholic might be the most misunderstood. Littauer (1992) describes melancholics as "the soul, the mind, the spirit, and the heart of humanity" (p. 44). How can these people who are often perceived as depressed introverts fit that description, you ask? Some characteristics that are not commonly associated with melancholics, but that are frequently present in their temperament, are their great sensitivity and compassion for others, and their creative, musical, or artistic talents and abilities.

The *peace* of the four temperaments is the **phlegmatic**. These are the people that everyone loves: even-tempered, cooperative, laid-back, easy going, and kind. Phlegmatics are not prone to extreme mood swings, are never in a hurry, and are not easily upset. They are considered to be good friends, dependable employees, and trustworthy ministers. They are generally good listeners and conflict mediators.

Certainly, phlegmatics have feelings, opinions, and emotions, just like everyone else. However, their temperament does not always allow for free expression of these. Phlegmatics are private with their thoughts and are generally introverted. They accept the ups and downs of life and work to stay in agreement with those in their circle.

Temperaments vs. Personalities

Oftentimes, temperaments and personalities are phrases that are used interchangeably. This is not accurate. Much like spiritual gifts (in the next chapter) are often mistaken for natural abilities (from chapter 5), personalities are often mistaken for natural temperaments.

Hal Warfield clearly and succinctly describes the difference this way: "Temperament differs from Personality in that Temperament is inborn and Personality grows out of upbringing, culture, family, and other external factors. Personality equals Temperament plus Life Experience" (Warfield, 2008, para. 1).

Personality = Temperament + Life Experience

I consider myself a perfect example of this. Remember when I shared with my pastor that I am a choleric sanguine? Well, technically, I am a melancholic sanguine by temperament. My natural temperament is equally introverted and extroverted. I am very analytical and artistic. I can be moody and I tend heavily toward perfectionism. I love being the center of attention, but I can't stay there too long without it fraying my introverted nerves. I love spending time alone, but the extroverted connector in me gets lonely fairly quickly. I love making people laugh, and I care deeply for other people, to the point of pain for myself. I will hug anyone and yes, I am prone to "bursts!"

I was born this way. I remember as a toddler alternating between asking my mom 101 questions, putting on my own plays and vocal performances, and crying because my mom wanted to give away my clothes. I wasn't concerned about my wardrobe because, as a part sanguine, I knew I would get more. I was concerned about how my clothes felt about being given away!

As I got older and entered the workforce, I turned into a total choleric. People were okay, but I was more interested in getting things done. I became a supervisor my first year of work because I couldn't stand NOT being the boss. I pursued administrative social work versus clinical work so that I could, indeed, be the boss. I excelled at work most when—surprise!—I was the boss. The more supervisors I had, the more miserable I was.

This choleric behavior was all in contrast to my naturally sensitive personality. I couldn't figure out why I felt like one person among my friends and family, and another person entirely at work. Authenticity is one of my primary values, so I knew that I was not being phony in one place or the other; I just could not put these two pictures of myself together. It was not until I began to research temperaments and personalities that I began to understand why and how that could be.

My personality is choleric sanguine, but my natural temperament is melancholic sanguine. Each spills over into the other occasionally to make a unique "me."

Why It Matters: Temperament Versus Personality

Why does the difference between temperament and personality matter? It matters both for getting to know each other better and for getting to know ourselves. As we know more about ourselves, we can learn more about the best ways for us to approach growing in our relationship with the Lord.

We are commanded to love the Lord and to love others. One of the ways to love others more easily is to understand them a bit better. How many times have we met people and made an instant judgment about them, only to later learn more about them and the reasons behind why they responded to everyday life and circumstances the way they did?

We may assume that a leader or a pastor is a friendly, people-loving extrovert. They are accessible, welcoming, and appear to enjoy spending time with people. As we get to know them outside of their roles, however, we may learn that they are born introverts.

While they like and appreciate people, they would much rather spend time by themselves or with a very select and small group of people who know them well. They may have to muster a significant amount of courage to speak up and speak out, to hire and fire people, to counsel, or to teach.

How does this happen? There are many causes. One of them is that what we are called or drawn to do in ministry, as a vocation or as a life role, may require us to demonstrate certain behaviors consistently. These behaviors, on the outside, are associated with certain temperaments—natural-born tendencies.

We may, however, be looking at the "mask" that people put on to fulfill their roles. For example, a very shy and introverted phlegmatic may have the talent to become a performing superstar. To be successful, she may have to put on the personality or temperament traits of a more sanguine personality. It is not her natural tendency, but it is within her ability to do so. We who are looking in from the outside may assume that her temperament is one of a sanguine, but in reality, we are looking at her created personality, one developed in response to a need.

What leads us to develop certain personalities, especially those that are different from our temperaments?

- **Influences** – We may be influenced by others in some way to behave differently than what comes naturally to us. We may need to hold our tongues in order to hold on to our jobs or to avoid emotional hurts. Whose behavior, examples, and expectations lead us to develop responses that are different than our natural temperament?
- **Experiences** – Our roles in life will definitely require us to behave differently than the way we were born. The question becomes, how much differently and how often? What in our work, social, academic, medical, legal, interpersonal, or developmental experience has drawn out of us behaviors that

are complementary or contrary to our natural temperament?
- **Values** – Values drive us to behave in ways that reflect what is most essential to us, even if these behaviors are not the most innate to us. What natural behaviors or priorities do we believe we need to change in order to adhere to those values that are most important to us?
- **Rewards/Punishments** – We are acknowledged by how closely we adhere to the expectations of others. From the time we are small children, we learn the social reward and punishment systems for our behaviors. How much of our behavior is in response to how others respond to it, both positively and negatively?
- **Requirements** – Goal-setting is the mark of progress and success. We may ask ourselves, "To get what I want and to move to where I want to be, how do I need to intentionally change my behavior (permanently or temporarily) outside of my own comfort zone?"

Temperaments Versus Christian Personalities

Authors Tim Lahaye and Florence Littauer have tackled the subject of temperaments and personality types, particularly as these relate to Christians.

Tim Lahaye's book, *Spirit Controlled Temperament* (1966), came first. In it, he explains that our temperament is a combination of genetic traits that we're born with, each with specific strengths and weaknesses that accompany these. No temperament is better or more desirable than the other, and these should only be used to assess ourselves, not necessarily to assess others.

One reason that temperaments should not be used to assess others, according to Lahaye, is because our temperaments are different from our personalities and our character. Our *personality* is the way we intentionally express ourselves outwardly to others.

Our *character* is the "real us," who we are when we are free to be ourselves, when others are not around to judge us. We may believe that we are assessing a person's temperament, but in reality, we are likely seeing his/her personality (what they show us) or character (what comes out when they are "pressed") (Lahaye, 1966).

Because we are born with natural temperament, Lahaye sees our temperaments as part of the "old man/old nature" that we have before accepting Christ (2 Corinthians 5:17). While temperaments do not change, Mr. Lahaye reminds us that the Holy Spirit may modify our temperaments in a way so that the weakness of these is minimized, and the strengths are maximized. We may appear to others as if our temperaments or personalities have changed, but the Lord has done a new thing (Isaiah 43:19) in us when this occurs. We are the same, but better (Lahaye, 1966).

Florence Littauer was highly inspired by Mr. Lahaye's book. A goal of Littauer's work was to move us beyond the labels of our personality and to help us to understand what to do with these. In other words, she wanted to provide an application that would help us to improve the quality of all of our relationships.

In her book, *Personality Plus* (1992), Littauer encourages her readers to understand the four temperaments and our unique blend of these before we try to change our personalities, or rather, "what shows on the surface" (Littauer, 1992, p. 11). She describes our temperaments as our true selves and our personalities as how we dress ourselves for others. She says:

> *My temperament is the real me; my personality is the dress I put on over me. I can look in the mirror in the morning and see a plain face, straight hair, and a bulgy body. That's the real me. Gratefully, within an hour I can apply makeup to create a colorful face; I can plug in the curling iron to fluff up my hair; and I can put on a flattering dress to camouflage too many curves. I've taken*

> *the real me and dressed it up, but I haven't permanently changed what's underneath.* (Littauer, 1992, pp. 11-12)

She posits that we can get along better with others by changing our personalities, and we can change our personalities when we understand our true selves or our temperaments better.

Littauer describes Tim LaHaye's book as a catalyst that helped her marriage. She said that she and her husband (who each have completely different temperaments) began to understand that "someone could be different and not be wrong" (p. 14).

Understanding the temperaments of a spouse, another loved one, a co-worker, or a co-laborer in Christ will help us to understand and accept their personalities as well, those parts of themselves that they show to us. Knowing more about them, and about ourselves and our temperaments, will help us to build more high quality relationships.

Understanding our temperaments and personalities will also help us build a stronger relationship with God. Marita Littauer (2005), Florence's daughter and fellow researcher, encourages us to identify the strengths in our personalities and to use these "as a springboard into our spiritual life: strengthening our relationship with God by maximizing our personality" (p. 31). She reiterates the point her mother makes about how understanding personalities can help us approach others differently and get along with them better. This is one way that we can love our neighbors, as Scripture states (Matthew 22:37-39) (Littauer, 2005).

From understanding our own personalities and those of others, we can:

- Have confidence in the way God has designed us and the unique way that this aspect of our design helps us to love Him;

- See the strengths that God has given us through our temperaments—strengths that can be used in our service to Him;
- Love our spouses more extravagantly by understanding their personalities and what they need in particular; and
- Find more fulfillment in various biblical mandates by understanding how we are created and by getting along better with others (Littauer, 2005).

Temperaments and Our Relationship with God

As an asset, God uses our temperaments as tools for how we relate to one another and to Him. Understanding how we are created helps us to see the best ways for us to develop a relationship with God. We can also work to build on the strengths of our personalities and minimize the weaknesses in our temperaments in order to serve better, have better relationships with others, meet the needs of others better, and reflect God's working in our lives.

For *phlegmatics* ("the peace"), God and your relationship with Him brings you great comfort. You more easily see God as a place of refuge and rest. Peaceful, orderly worship services that do not require much individual participation are where you thrive. An understanding of God's sovereignty is a spiritual strength of yours. You are likely to enjoy spending time with God in prayer, meditation, and study that is unrushed and unscripted. You easily exhibit the Christ-like qualities that we are most encouraged to emulate: humility, service, compassion, fairness, and peace (Littauer, 2005).

To reflect greater dependence on God and confidence in your relationship with Him, phlegmatics can:

- Be more bold and strong in service and in contributions (Joshua 1:6);

- Be more confident and fearless in demonstrating love for others and for God (2 Timothy 1:7); and
- Reflect more genuine enthusiasm (Colossians 3:23) (Carbonell, n.d.).

For *cholerics* ("the boss"), seeing the Lord as controlling is most common. As cholerics, you are likely to want to emulate God's control or to battle with Him for it in your own life. In worship, you are likely to focus on the teaching. Your works on behalf of the Lord are very important because you are by nature very productive. You are likely to demonstrate your faith by keeping busy and active in serving. In your process of growing closer to God, you are likely to be goal-oriented: you want to see results, and soon. Like Jesus, you are comfortable as a leader, focused on your goal and purpose, and you are always taking definitive action (Littauer, 2005).

To reflect power, strength, and growth in your relationship with God and others, cholerics should concentrate on:

- Being more gentle and sincere in their interactions with others, and less directive or "bossy" (James 3:17);
- Controlling negative outbursts and actions, and not holding grudges (Ephesians 4:26);
- Focusing on one thing at a time and staying in the present, understanding that this actually boosts productivity and the quality of your services (Philippians 3:13); and
- Developing a genuine heart for service to others, knowing that the purpose of your expertise is to help other people and be a blessing to them (Galatians 5:13) (Carbonell, n.d.)

For *melancholics* ("the brains"), being in touch with the fear of the Lord comes most naturally. You are likely to appreciate the structure and predictability as the most important aspect of worship service. Your spiritual strength is in knowledge: you want to not only know God more, but to know the why of things. You thrive on the structure of the spiritual disciplines. However, be sure that you are truly worshiping the Lord rather than just worshiping the habits of prayer, Bible reading, journaling, etc. Like Jesus, you are uniquely sensitive to the needs of other people. Also, like Jesus, you are likely to be smarter than everyone else around you, as well as mature and wise beyond your years and experience (Littauer, 2005).

To reflect your Christ-like qualities, melancholics should:

- Think positively toward others and toward God (Philippians 4:8);
- Avoid being critical and negative (Romans 14:10-14), and concentrate on encouraging others whenever possible;
- Purpose to be joyful! Reflect happiness, gladness, and positivity as a response to what God has done in your life (Galatians 5:22); and
- Decide not to worry, fret, and stress out (Psalm 37:1) (Carbonell, n.d.)

For *sanguines* ("the stars"), viewing God as your friend and a loving Father comes naturally. Sanguines see everyone as friendly and in their corner! Church participation that includes entertaining sermons and great fellowship is where you thrive. Each day is fresh and new to you, so you are in touch with God's grace as a source of spiritual strength for you. The spiritual disciplines are a struggle for you, because discipline in general is a struggle! It is important that you find processes that work best for you, not those that are prescribed by others. Like Jesus, you are an energetic, optimistic, "follow me" magnet, and you've never met a stranger (Littauer, 2005).

While you are generally positive, you can grow further in reflecting God's glory in your life and in blessing others by:

The GOD ASSETS: God's Investment in You and What to Do With It

- Avoiding pride and remaining humble (James 3:17) by remembering that loving God and loving others is our commandment;
- Controlling your tongue (Psalm 141:3), remembering not to say everything you think or tell everything you know in your eagerness to connect with others;
- Being more organized (1 Corinthians 14:40) with your schedule, tasks, and belongings so that these do not distract or hinder others; and
- Being patient (Galatians 5:23), an important fruit of the Spirit (Carbonell, n.d.).

Coaching Questions

- Which of the temperaments best describe the real you?
- What are the characteristics of your temperament, the inborn, natural components of how you think, feel, behave, and see the world?
- What are the characteristics of your most dominant personality, the behaviors you "put on" for the world as needed? Which of the temperaments best describe your dominant personality?
- How closely related are your temperament and your personality? Is this a good thing or a bad thing?
- What is the single most important thing you can begin to do now to maximize the positive aspects of your temperament, minimize the negative aspects, and better reflect your love for God and others?
- If your GOD ASSETS were the recipe to your favorite dish, what ingredient would your temperament be? Why is that so?

CHAPTER 10
SPIRITUAL GIFTS

Each of the people we have been following has a specific set of strengths, talents, abilities, passions, and characteristics that make them stand out in their own special way. They are also Christians of varying levels of commitment and maturity, and are endowed with specific spiritual abilities designed to help them serve the body of Christ more effectively. These spiritual abilities, or spiritual gifts, are also used by them in their professional and personal lives consciously and unconsciously.

Amber—our worker with performance troubles—has some hidden spiritual gifts. She has prayed fervently for the success of Liz's nonprofit. She has also helped to raise a significant amount of money in donations and has solicited a high number of volunteers. Unfortunately, praying, fundraising, and volunteer recruitment are not in her job description! She is gifted as an intercessor and an evangelist, but these spiritual gifts are not a clear match for the tasks she is assigned at her office.

Rachel, Amber's supervisor, and Liz, the nonprofit CEO and founder, are both gifted in the areas of leadership and administration. Leaders perceive ideals and lead others to success; administrators organize people and resources for maximum efficiency and effectiveness. These spiritual gifts help them to be successful in their professional lives because the gifts are a good match for the responsibilities of their positions. Each of them has different secondary gifts that help them relate to people differently, which explains their different responses and interactions with Amber.

Liz's father, William, is also a spiritually gifted leader. He is also gifted as an exhorter or encourager. He has a supernatural ability, given by God, to strengthen, advise, and counsel people to help them live up to their full potential at work and in Christ. John, the descendant of William's company's founder, gives William the blues not only because of a personal sense of entitlement, but because of an administrative spiritual gift use gone awry. Because John's prayer and devotional life is minimal and his participation in church is limited, he does not have that internal "tug" that others feel in terms of how he approaches challenges and problems on the job.

Susan, Liz's mother and William's wife, is gifted in the area of hospitality. She throws the best parties and has never met a stranger. She, too, has an administrative gift, a natural, God-given tendency to see order and structure and help it to come to pass. But don't sleep on Susan and assume that she is all smiles and photo ops—Susan also has strong spiritual gifts in the areas of discernment, prophecy, and intercession. On more than one occasion, her prayerful petitions and the revelations she has received and shared with her husband have helped William to make the types of decisions on the job that drive John crazy! In the end, these decisions have always brought success to the company or helped the company avoid a potential disaster that no one else saw coming.

Liz wishes her mom would "get a word" for her on how to handle her meddling and controlling CFO, Chris. Chris has a choleric primary temperament and a melancholic secondary temperament. While the melancholic in him is made for work such as long-range planning and finances, his choleric temperament leads him to push to be in charge. Spiritually, his gift of teaching makes him appear bossy *rather than informative. He is not as strong spiritually in the area of administration, which makes him more disorganized in terms of his tasks and schedule than Liz would like. An irritating employee with mediocre job performance is a dangerous combination!*

Research shows us that while our temperaments and our spiritual gifts are very different, these inform each other and work together to create the unique aspects of each of us (Spiritual Gifts Research, 2007).

Spiritual Gifts as an Asset

This asset is perhaps the closest to my heart. As I explained in the Introduction of the book, it is the revelation of spiritual gifts that brought me to the arena of writing, teaching, speaking, coaching, and entrepreneurship.

As God was ministering to me, I understood that this slice of information, this one, essential ingredient in a recipe, would help so many Christians to understand and decide one of the key purposes for which we exist. If we really knew and truly believed that God gifted us uniquely and had a purpose and a call for each of us, how much backsliding might we avoid? How many people would stay in church and not leave? How many people would remain in the faith and not recant? How many people would remain faithful to the ministries they serve, and not constantly change and leave needs unmet? How might it free people to love God and serve others, rather than constantly focusing on our own needs and ourselves?

On its own, understanding what our spiritual gifts are is an asset unto itself!

About Spiritual Gifts

The Bible does not specifically define spiritual gifts. However, it describes them in enough detail for us to understand what they are and how these are to be used.

> *A spiritual gift is the God-given capacity of every Christian to carry out his [or her] function in the body of Christ.* – (Deffinbaugh, 2004, under *Purpose of Spiritual Gifts,* para.1)

A spiritual gift is defined or described as empowering:

> *A Spiritual Gift is a special divine empowerment bestowed on each believer by the Holy Spirit to accomplish a given ministry, God's way, according to His grace and discernment, to be used within the context of the Body of Christ.* – (Ministry Tools Resource Center, para. 3)

In short, your spiritual gifts are your superpowers!

Why Do Our Spiritual Gifts Matter?

Well, if God gives you a superpower, you can bet it has great value and an important reason for existing! That should be enough.

Here are a few other reasons why it is important for us to understand all of the spiritual gifts and to know our own:

- The Bible says they are important by devoting several key passages of Scripture to them (1 Corinthians 12, 1 Corinthians 14, Romans 12, 1 Peter 4, Ephesians 4).
- Our spiritual gifts are a key indication of God's will and purpose for our lives, since we are expected to use them in service to Him and to others (1 Peter 4). Using our gifts properly and effectively will help us demonstrate our love for others and our reverence for God.
- Understanding our gifts helps us to set service priorities. If we have gifts, we are to use those (Romans 12:6-8). We

should not spend significant amounts of time on tasks and responsibilities that do not allow us to utilize our spiritual gifts.
- We must be diligent stewards over what God gives us, including our gifts (1 Peter 4:10).
- Using our gifts helps us to experience a true fulfillment in our purpose and in our service. Your spiritual gifts are a key ingredient in God's unique recipe for YOU! Failing to activate this ingredient will leave you feeling incomplete and out of alignment with what God has called you to do.

If you want to know how you function and why, identifying your primary spiritual gift and the characteristics of that gift will be revelatory. If you want to find true fulfillment in your Christian ministry and in your life, knowing what your spiritual gift is and focusing your ministry around that gift is the way to go.

What are the Spiritual Gifts?
(Hickey, 1986; Carraway, 2005)

There are three primary groupings of gifts in the Bible:

1. Gifts of the Spirit (1 Corinthians 12)
2. Five-fold ministry gifts (Ephesians 4)
3. Motivational or foundational gifts (Romans 12)

Gifts of the Spirit – from 1 Corinthians 12

Discernment	Miracles
Faith	Prophecy
Healing	Tongues
Interpretation of Tongues	Word of Knowledge
	Word of Wisdom

The GOD ASSETS: God's Investment in You and What to Do With It

Five-Fold Ministry Gifts – from Ephesians 4	Motivational or Foundational Gifts – from Romans 12
Apostle	Prophecy
Prophet	Serving
Evangelist	Teaching
Pastor or Shepherd	Exhortation or Encouraging
Teacher	Giving
	Administration, Organizing, or Leading
	Mercy

Other Spiritual Gifts

The Bible also mentions the spiritual gifts of speaking, serving, and hospitality in 1 Peter 4:9-11. These are understood by some to be duplications of gifts mentioned earlier. Speaking would be considered the gift of prophecy, and serving is mentioned in Romans.

Other gifts are mentioned in various places in the Bible. The Old Testament mentions craftsmanship, interpretation of dreams, and worship as spiritual endowments. Other gifts mentioned in the New Testament include deliverance, intercession, missionary, martyrdom, and simplicity.

1 Peter 4:9-11	Old Testament	New Testament
Speaking (Prophecy)	Craftsmanship	Deliverance
Serving	Interpretation of Dreams	Intercession
Hospitality	Worship	Missionary
		Martyrdom
		Simplicity

Spiritual Gift Categories

Other than by Scripture passage, another way to categorize the gifts is by function:

- *Sign gifts:* deliverance, healing, miracles, martyrdom, prophecy, tongues
- *Ministry gifts:* administration, craftsmanship, discernment, exhortation, faith, giving, helps, hospitality, intercession, interpretation of dreams, interpretation of tongues, leadership, mercy, missionary, serving, simplicity, word of knowledge, word of wisdom, worship
- *Foundational gifts:* apostle, evangelist, pastor, prophet, teacher

(Yes, these "foundational gifts" are different than the other group. These are not official categories. They are just ways to understand the many gifts that God provides in the body of Christ.)

The easiest and most helpful way to break the gifts down (for me) is into two categories:

1. *Speaking Gifts:* Those involved primarily with proclaiming a truth verbally or in writing

2. *Serving Gifts:* Those involved primarily with serving and ministering with strength and action

Speaking Gifts (Proclaiming Truth)	Serving Gifts (Ministering with Power)
Administration/Leadership	Craftsmanship
Evangelism	Deliverance
Exhortation	Discernment
Interpretation of Tongues	Faith
Prophet	Giving
Prophecy	Healing
Teaching	Helps
Tongues	Hospitality
Word of Knowledge	Intercession
Word of Wisdom	Interpretation of dreams
	Martyrdom
	Mercy
	Miracles
	Missionary
	Serving
	Simplicity
	Worship

Primary Gifts, Secondary Gifts, and Gift Mixes

Each person has at least one **primary** spiritual gift—your ultimate spiritual superpower. Through a combination of gifts assessment, feedback from spiritually mature people, and your own assessment, identifying this gift is a relatively straightforward process. This process may take some time and may not be evident until a believer is more spiritually mature. Indications of this gift are evident in a person's life experiences, even before they become a Christian.

Some people also have **secondary** spiritual gifts. These gifts may not be as clear and strong as a primary gift; however, they are still evident. For example, a person may have a primary spiritual gift of prophecy or perceiving, but a teaching or encouraging gift may also be strong for them. Secondary gifts can be very strong and supportive of a person's primary spiritual gift. These usually go very well together in ministry.

Your **gift mix** is the collective group of primary and secondary gifts, plus other gifts in which you are strong, if this is applicable. For example, two people may have the gift of giving, but one may give more monetarily and the other may be more apt to donate goods. Looking at their gift mix, one may be more service-oriented (task support), and the other may be more helps-oriented (people support).

Supernatural empowerments of varying degrees show up in your recipe.

"My" Gifts vs. the "Other" Gifts: Being vs. Doing

Here is a truth that most teachers, churches, and books do not share: every Christian will be called to minister in every major area of spiritual giftedness at some point. Some exceptions to the everyone/all gifts rule would be "exceptional" gifts such as martyrdom or craftsmanship.

We are all called on and required in Scripture as Christ-followers to be ready to serve in whatever capacity whenever there is someone in need. Those who do not have the gift of teaching will be called on to instruct others. Those who may not have musicality or particular artistic talents are still called on to worship and may be sometimes in a position to lead. People who are more spiritually gifted in helps (people-centered) ministry can bet on being called on to provide more task-centered support (service ministry).

For this reason, it is important that we learn not only about our own gifts or superpowers, but about the other gifts as well. We must also learn the Scriptures that coincide with those gifts, and how the Holy Spirit is leading and teaching each of us to serve at any time. This is in preparation for "doing" those gifts that we are not spiritually empowered in "being."

In coaching, we discuss the concept of "being" versus "doing." Oftentimes, we focus on doing to get a particular outcome. We may ask, "What do I need to do to get out of this situation or to get what I want?" In reality, focusing on developing a key characteristic (or focusing on "being") is what helps to bring about lasting change and facilitates more permanent, positive impact.

It's the same with our spiritual superpowers. When we serve in the areas where we are strongly spiritually gifted, we are *being* who God made us. We are serving in an area of spiritual strength. As we serve and rely more on God, our gift will get stronger and become more evident.

We want to be sure in ministry that we are spending a majority of time in our being areas of spiritually-gifted strength. Our church services should be focused on ministries that require us to draw on our true areas of spiritual giftedness. While we may serve in other areas as needed, our focus of energy, time, commitment, and dedication should not be here.

Consider the Pareto Principle, better known as the 80/20 Rule. We often hear it applied in group work and volunteer settings—that 20 percent of the people do 80 percent of the work. We also hear this in terms of our daily tasks: that 20 percent of our work requires 80 percent of our resources and that we only spend about 20 percent of our time on what is truly most important. To be most effective in ministry and service, we want to reverse this principle. We should be spending 80 percent of our ministry time in areas in which we are very strongly spiritually gifted (being), and the other 20 percent of time in areas where we have complementary gifts or where we are needed (doing).

Spiritual Gifts vs. Everything Else

How do you know if a "power" that you have is a spiritual gift, a talent, a natural strength, or developed by experience?

The answer is not always cut and dried, and frankly, it's not always important. What we need to know is how we are fashioned, wired, empowered, and put together—the ingredients in our own unique recipe. After that, we need to put all these ingredients to use in full force in leadership and service to others.

Here is an example of how spiritual gifts may look like other parts of our makeup, or GOD ASSETS.

Nicole (That's Me)

I have been told frequently that I have the "gift" of administration. Well, there are a few challenges with that.

Let's unpack "administration" a bit. Here are some of the characteristics of that gift:

1. A "born leader" (who does not exist—see chapter 7)
2. Is a clear communicator
3. Is able to visualize a big picture and longer-range goals
4. Takes pleasure in setting and achieving stated goals
5. Has great spiritual insight into delegation
6. Is aware of the available resources to complete a task
7. Likes to be busy all the time
8. Is task-oriented rather than people-oriented

9. Will endure being criticized in order to complete a task, assignment, or goal
10. Prefers to be under authority rather than to have authority
11. Will only assume authority if none exists
12. Appreciates, respects, and needs structure and order
13. Will allow others to take credit in order to meet a goal
14. Great zeal and enthusiasm for their task or goal
15. Note-taker who writes notes to his or herself
16. Wants to move on to a new goal once the first one is accomplished
17. Wants to see things completed as quickly as possible
18. Does not enjoy routine tasks
19. Enjoys working with people

I see a lot of myself in this description. However, is "administration" really a spiritual gift of mine? Here are some considerations:

- People with other spiritual gifts share many of these same characteristics. For example, perceivers/prophets are also willing to be criticized for a greater goal (#9); servers are big on order (#12); and teachers are more content-oriented or goal-oriented than people-oriented (#8). Perhaps I have one of those gifts instead?
- Some of these characteristics are also in line with my temperament, my values, my abilities/strengths, my leadership style, and my experiences. For example, my primary **temperament** type is melancholic, so note taking, list making, and task orientation come with that. Connectedness and strategic thinking are two of my top **strengths**, so resource identification, long-range planning, and goal setting are integral to those. In my career, I have always gravitated toward job responsibilities that are more governing, overseeing, and ***task-oriented,*** and I excel in these. Might some of my strengths in the area of administration come from these other GOD ASSETS?

- There are some key positive characteristics of administrators that I lack. For example, one of my primary values is liberty. I do NOT like having a boss (!), so #10 is out for me. I also admit that others taking and receiving credit for something that I did and accomplished (#13) is a pet peeve of mine. (I try to do a good job of also giving credit where credit is due in return.)
- While I lack some key positive characteristics, all of the areas for improvement or awareness are part of me! I get frustrated when people on my team and in my corner don't seem to share my same goals. Others perceive me as being a bit callous sometimes because of the criticism I take in work (#9 above). I have been known to focus so intently on work and quality that I don't take a breath to see that other people have lives beyond my goal. I have, in the past, neglected myself, my personal relationships, and even basic chores and responsibilities to focus on a goal. (I have since been delivered—being a good coach and all.)
- Frankly, I don't love administration. I may be able to complete aspects of it in my sleep, but I don't enjoy it. For example, administrators are admonished to always explain why they are doing something or implementing a process and to take more time with people individually to get them on board. That, I admit, is not a strong suit of ministry. I am great, however, at encouraging people to utilize their own natural and spiritual gifts to accomplish what I have delegated. I use the spiritual gift of encouragement or exhortation to do so.

On spiritual gifts assessments (of which I have taken MANY, MANY, MANY!), I score middle-high in administration or leadership. It is not my primary gift or a strong secondary gift; however, it is clearly part of my gift mix.

Even if administration is not a particular spiritual gift of mine and even if I don't love it, I should still use it if it's needed in ministry or if it will be helpful to one of my goals. Even if I can't "be" an administrator, I can "do" administration.

Superpowers in Everyday Action

Some people are just born with a leg up. Evangelism, faith, giving, and hospitality are great examples of areas that we can all get better in with effort and practice. People who have these spiritual gifts—supernatural endowment in these areas—demonstrate a level of excellence and expertise that is uncommon compared to those of us who are working to improve at it through skill-building.

Some of us have spiritual superpowers in these areas. Christians who have these spiritual gifts or supernatural powers in these areas can tell because these responsibilities come very naturally, easily, and consistently to them. Participating in activities that reflect these gifts gives them joy. Spiritually gifted Christians don't really struggle too much in their areas of giftedness, and they are eager to serve in these areas at any time.

My husband is a gifted evangelist. He loves God, loves the Word, and has never met a stranger. He's the guy in the convenience store who always says hello, is ready with an encouraging word, and asks you within two minutes of meeting you where you go to church. He's led people to the Lord on the playground, and I've seen him hold up medical procedures while his witness to the power of Christ holds medical personnel completely captive. It's awe-inspiring—and I say this not just because he's my sweetie! He is "being" an evangelist all the time. I, on the other hand, must muster up the courage and work hard to "do" evangelism with strangers.

R.G. LeTourneau is best known for his act of faith in living off of 10 percent of his business earnings and giving 90 percent as a "reverse tithe" to God (Great Christians in Business, n.d.). While this is credited to Mr. LeTourneau's faith, this idea was actually the suggestion of his wife, Evelyn. Such an idea does not come out of nowhere: it has to be inspired by God. Mrs. LeTourneau was clearly a spiritually gifted giver and a woman of great faith.

We may see such a decision as easy for someone of significant means, but our gifts are with us from birth. No matter how much money her family business would have earned, Evelyn is likely to have given sacrificially for the cause of Christ. She was built that way. Such a supernatural empowerment was in God's recipe for her, for His purposes. Evelyn LeTourneau's obedience to that vision and that gift is now a legacy for Christians everywhere. Most famously, Pastor Rick Warren and his wife, Kay, currently live on a reverse tithe. They take no salary from Saddleback Church and live off of 10 percent of the earnings they make from books, speaking engagements, and other activities.

Spiritual Gifts vs. Duties

These gifts may receive little credit or attention because Scripture tells all Christians to share their faith, to stand in faith, to be hospitable to others, and to give sacrificially. We have a Christian duty and responsibility to do these things.

As far as the gifts of evangelism, faith, hospitality, and giving, we may think or say, "Oh, so what? Rich people giving! Christians witnessing! What's new about that?" or "What kind of Christian has no faith?"

If the Bible has to tell us to do something or not to do something, then it means that "something" does not come naturally to a majority of us. If having faith in God constantly (Mark 11:22), tithing and giving (Malachi 3:10; Luke 6:38; 2 Corinthians 9:6-8), being hospitable (Hebrews 13:1-2; Romans 12:13), and evangelizing (John 10:16; Acts 1:8; Philemon 6) were easy and natural, we would not need encouragement, admonishment, directives, and examples to do these or be these.

All of us are encouraged and required as Christians to complete the primary responsibilities of these areas as duties. With practice, we become proficient at most of these actions. Along the way, we may struggle frequently or even always. If these are not our spiritual gifts, we may feel convicted, stressed, or possibly resentful when trying to fulfill biblical mandates in these areas.

Christians who are not supernaturally empowered in these areas might seek out those who are gifted for advice on how to be better in these areas, because for most of us, these are not cakewalks. Setting out a spread for twenty-five people on short notice (with joy, no less!), staying in faith for supernatural deliverances, witnessing to strangers, and giving of our money and time sacrificially, time and time again, does not come easy for the majority of people.

The lack of ease in performance doesn't mean that we are not good Christians. It means that we are dependent on an all-powerful God and on His people, who He has empowered to set the example for the rest of us.

Most of us need help in these areas. However, Scripture and direction for these make people who have spiritual gifts and superpowers in these areas smile! They make it all look totally easy! Spiritually gifted evangelists, faith walkers, givers, and hospitality leaders are ready to encourage others to do the same and to teach other people how it's done. They often utter the phrase, "It's simple!" when explaining how a Christian should follow these mandates.

It does not mean that these are without effort. For example, even the most passionate and hospitable person has a bad day occasionally and may not be in the best mood to receive company.

I'm sure that givers and faith walkers have to lean into the Lord and push themselves beyond comfort to continue to give and to serve when there are financial or other challenges in their lives.

What Are My Gifts?

Some spiritual gifts are more easily discerned than others. To get started right away understanding what your gifts are, here are some steps you can take:

1. **Prayer.** The One Who made you will not withhold information from you! Pray and ask God to reveal to you what your gifts are. You may receive an answer to prayer right away, or your answer may become clear from following more of the steps below.

2. **Word and study.** Review the Scriptures that describe or outline the spiritual gifts. Do some study on your own to begin to better understand the spiritual gifts. You may begin to understand how you are gifted simply by understanding the gifts themselves.

3. Take a **spiritual gifts inventory.** One of the most popular ones can be found at www.SpiritualGiftsTest.com. There are adult and youth versions of this free, online test.

4. Take several **different inventories.** Each test or inventory assesses for a different set of gifts. If the same two or three gifts continue to rise to the top in your tests, you can be fairly certain that these are strong areas of gifting for you.

5. Remember that inventories are only the beginning! Ask others to **confirm** or verify what you've learned from the steps above. Each gift identified should be easily verifiable by:

    a) People who know you well
    b) Spiritually mature Christians
    c) Confirmation within yourself

6. **Life review.** Doing a review of significant life information can often lend clues to which of the spiritual gifts you are empowered to use. You can consider things you were interested in doing as a child; your own natural temperament; your areas of drive, devotion, and desire; your abilities and strengths; and things at work, home, or in volunteering that come most naturally and easily to you. A picture of your spiritual gifts may emerge.

7. **Needs identification.** Are there certain needs that seem to appear every time you show up? This may be an indication of what your spiritual gifts are. For example, over a period of several years in my work, I found myself taking over in leadership for several women whose styles were very different from my own. Because they led with a certain style, some key things that needed to happen on the job were missing. My primary spiritual gifts kicked in to fill those gaps, aided by my leadership style. When I left those leadership positions, people with spiritual gifts different than my own replaced me to fill the gaps that my own leadership style and supernatural areas of strength had left for them.

Don't wait—take action to identify your spiritual gifts right now! You will begin to be more fulfilled right away as you strategize ways to exercise these gifts at church, in your community, in your home, at work, and everywhere!

Coaching Questions:

- What does your church teach you about spiritual gifts?
- How does your church's teaching affect the way you think about spiritual gifts?
- If you have been taught that some gifts are not in use anymore, but you learn through the steps above that you have that gift, what would happen? What would you do?

- Do you know what your gift is? If so, are you using it regularly and effectively? If not, why not?
- What is one step you can take today to begin learning more about your spiritual gifts?
- If your GOD ASSETS were the recipe to your favorite dish, what ingredient would your spiritual gifts be? Why is that so?

The GOD ASSETS: God's Investment in You and What to Do With It

Conclusion

What's Cooking? Where to Go Next

Thank you for taking the time to read this book. My prayer is that a few things were accomplished:

1. That you have begun to **know yourself better**—why you are who you are and why you do some of the things you do (Psalm 139:14-16; Hosea 4:6; John 8:32; 1 Corinthians 2:14; 2 Corinthians 12:9-10; 2 Corinthians 13:5; Ephesians 2:10)
2. That you have begun to **identify and appreciate more of God's handiwork** in your life—and that this identification leads to **gratitude** to Him (Genesis 1:27; Jeremiah 31:3; Matthew 10:29-31; Hebrews 4:12)
3. That your **faith in God's great plan for you and for your life has increased**—and that you are **spurred on to more action** (Romans 12:1-2; 2 Timothy 1:6-7; Hebrews 11:1)
4. That **God's plan for your work life and ministry has been revealed or confirmed**—and that you are **ready to move forward with confidence** (John 8:36; John 10:10; 2 Timothy 1:6-7; 1 Peter 2:9)

If you have been on a responsible eating plan, I hope all this recipe talk has not thrown you off!

If you hate to cook, would rather not cook, don't know how to cook, or just avoid cooking like the plague, I can relate! I hope that reading this book will give you some inspiration to cook more—with love, joy, and an eye to replicating God's love in your life. If people in your life ask why you smile now when cooking or even planning to cook, tell them why—you're considering God's recipe in your own life!

Next Steps

So now that you have some new revelation (or confirmation of what you've known all along), where do you go with it? What do you do with it?

Pray

This is a lot of information to take in all at once. Ask God what He would have you take away from the book right now and how He would like you to apply it to your life, work, and ministry in the immediate future.

Peruse

Check out the GOD ASSETS blog! The link to the blog can be found on The God Assets web page at www.TheGodAssets.com. There are regular video, audio, picture, and recipe posts! (Regular old posts in writing pop up as well.) Follow the blog and receive new posts via email or in your blog reader (Feedly, Blog Lovin', Blogger Reading List, etc.). New posts are put up regularly, and each post is archived conveniently for review.

Personal Support

Do you have a friend, colleague, sister, or co-worker who would benefit from this book? Get her (or him!) a copy, or send your buddy to the website at TheGodAssets.com to order. As your partners read the book, discuss with them what they are learning and share what you have learned as well. Once each of you decides to take action, encourage and support each other through accountability.

Choose your personal support partners wisely! Be sure they are people in whom you can truly trust with confidence and people who are likely to follow through with support.

Perks! (More) Perks!
Based on the leading of God and the expressed needs of readers, I will be making empowerment service offerings available in the near future. As an "early adopter" (you got the book!), you can begin thinking about which of these offerings might serve you best. These offerings require various investment levels of time, treasure, and toil (yep, we have some work to do!). I promise that each will be *fun*, and that you will experience *joy* with them all.

Upcoming Offerings

Portable – The Coach-on-the-Go Series

Coaching on each of the components of GOD ASSETS is delivered to you in audio coaching format, with worksheets and assessments to help you along the way.

Partner with Peers – The 12-Month Membership Program

Would you like some guidance on how each of these assets can be identified and activated in your life for maximum personal fulfillment and maximum kingdom impact? The upcoming membership program is just for you! Stay tuned.

The GOD ASSETS: God's Investment in You and What to Do With It

Power and Progress – The 91-Day Group Coaching Intensive

Are you ready to move forward in a major way with the vision that God has given you? The GOD ASSETS 13-week Group Coaching Intensive will help give you that sense of clear direction and Spirit-based strength. The intensive helps you focus and implement these principles in a timely fashion, with the help of others who are similarly committed and motivated to make a big kingdom impact!

Potent and Private – The Individual Coaching Program

If one-on-one attention is what you need, then the individual coaching program will work best for you. This is a multi-session, renewable program that aligns with the GOD ASSETS book. We take a close look at where you are, where you would like to go, and what God is saying to you, specifically. After private coaching, you will have a much clearer vision of your unique GOD ASSETS and how these should be activated in your work, life, and ministry.

Premier – The V.I.P. Intensive

Like dinner, some things need to be delivered in a hurry! The VIP Intensive is designed for people like me who have no patience, or for people who are tired of waiting or stalling and are ready to make bold moves NOW!

The VIP Intensive is a full day or half-day intensive coaching session. By the end of a VIP session, you will have a complete plan of action, specific action steps with timelines, accountability and support plans, resources needed and identified, and a new appreciation of how much God loves you and how good His plan is for you.

Present – The GOD ASSETS Workshop

My sanguine sister (from chapter 9) says that all she has to do to find me is to look no further than the nearest women's retreat. I say she might be right—except I just might travel to the farthest retreat, too!

The GOD ASSETS program can be brought to your church or organization for retreats and trainings. Working through the material together as a team can help members understand each other better and can help the team strategize how to work together much more effectively.

Full weekend, full day, half-day, and single session options are available.

Again, more information is available at the website at www.TheGodAssets.com.

Please don't let this be another book that you have enjoyed reading but that sits on your shelf or in your Kindle or other eReader with the others. It is meant to be used, referenced, dog-eared, and shared with others who also want to know what they can do to live more fulfilled lives.

So, the answer is yes—yes, your food is ready! Calorie free. Eat and enjoy!

> *Open your mouth and taste, open your eyes and see—how good GOD is. Blessed are you who run to him.* – Psalm 34:8 in *The Message Bible (MSG)*

The GOD ASSETS: God's Investment in You and What to Do With It

Notes and References

Introduction: Why GOD ASSETS?

Hickey, M. (1986). *Know Your Ministry*. Denver, CO: Marilyn Hickey Ministries.

Chapter 1: The GOD ASSETS: God's Unique Recipe for YOU!

Highfield, R. (2002, December 20). "DNA survey finds all humans 99 percent the same." *The Telegraph*. Retrieved from http://www.telegraph.co.uk/news/worldnews/northamerica/usa/1416706/DNA-survey-finds-all-humans-are-99.9pc-the-same.html

The Smithsonian National Museum of Natural History. (n.d.). "What does it mean to be human?" Retrieved from http://humanorigins.si.edu/evidence/genetics

Chapter 2: God and faith

Easton, M. G. (1897). *Faith*. New York, N.Y.: Thomas Nelson Publishers. Retrieved from http://www.biblestudytools.com/dictionaries/eastons-bible-dictionary/faith.html

Faith. In (1996). W. Elwell (Ed.), *Baker's Evangelical Dictionary of Biblical Theology*. Grand Rapids, MI: Baker Book House Company. Retrieved from http://www.biblestudytools.com/dictionaries/bakers-evangelical-dictionary/faith.html

Faith. (2011). In *Merriam-Webster.com*. Retrieved from http://www.merriam-webster.com/dictionary/faith?show=0&t=1379521569

Faith. (n.d.). *Encyclopedia Britannica, Inc.* Retrieved December 20, 2013, from http://dictionary.reference.com/browse/faith

Faith. (n.d.). *Roget's 21st Century Thesaurus, Third Edition.* Retrieved from http://thesaurus.com/browse/faith

Fortune, D. & Fortune, K. (1987). *Discover Your God-Given Gifts.* Grand Rapids, MI: Chosen Books.

Chapter 3: Overriding Values

Brownson, T. (2010). *What Are My Values?* Retrieved from http://www.adaringadventure.com/life-coaching/what-are-my-values/

Brownson, T. (2013). *Core Values.* Retrieved from http://www.coachthelifecoach.com/core-values/.

Johnson, S.M. (2011). Do Not Make a Career Decision Without This List. Retrieved from http://developmentcrossroads.com/2011/08/career-decision-list/

Chapter 4: Drive, Desire, Devotion, and Dedication

Dedicate. (2013). *Merriam-Webster.com.* Retrieved from http://www.merriam-webster.com/dictionary/dedicate

Desire. (2013). *Merriam-Webster.com.* Retrieved from http://www.merriam-webster.com/dictionary/desire

Devote. (2013). *Merriam-Webster.com.* Retrieved from http://www.merriam-webster.com/dictionary/devote

Drive. (2013.) *Merriam-Webster.com.* Retrieved from http://www.merriam-webster.com/dictionary/drive

Lyles, J. *Youth 10x's Better Mission Statement.* Retrieved from http://youth10xbetter.org/home.php

Warren, R. (2002). *The Purpose-Driven Life.* Grand Rapids, MI: Zondervan.

Chapter 5: Abilities and Strengths

Cookthink LLC. (n.d.) "What is a leavener?" Retrieved from http://www.cookthink.com/reference/1946/What_is_a_leavener.

Gallup. (2013). "What is the Clifton Strengthsfinder?" Retrieved from http://strengths.gallup.com/help/general/125525/Clifton-StrengthsFinder.aspx.

McGinnis, T. (2007). "The four StrengthsFinder domains." Retrieved from http://cliftonstrengthsfinder.blogspot.com/2007/01/strengths-finder-themes-categories.html.

McGinnis, T. (2009). "New Domains according to 'Strengths-Based Leadership.'" Retrieved from http://cliftonstrengthsfinder.blogspot.com/2009/02/new-domains-according-to-strengths.html

Rath, T. (2007). *StrengthsFinder 2.0.* New York, NY: Gallup Press.

Reveal Ventures, LLC. (n.d.) "Strengthsfinder Leadership Themes." Retrieved from http://www.strengthstest.com/strengthsfinderthemes/leadership-themes.html

Chapter 6: Style of Conflict

Bonnan-White, J. (2013). *Style Matters Presentation: Communication and Conflict Based on the Kraybill Conflict Style Inventory.* Retrieved from http://prezi.com/lc3bel3ddtjg/style-matters-presentation-dr-jess-bonnan-white/

conflict. (n.d.). *Dictionary.com Unabridged.* Retrieved from http://dictionary.reference.com/browse/conflict

Conflict. (2013). In *Merriam-Webster.com.* Retrieved from http://www.merriam-webster.com/dictionary/conflict.

conflict. (n.d.). *Roget's 21st Century Thesaurus, Third Edition.* Retrieved from http://thesaurus.com/browse/conflict

Consulting Psychologists Press, Inc. (2001). *Thomas-Kilmann Conflict Mode Instrument, Profile and Interpretive Report: Michaels Pat (sample).* Retrieved from *https://www.skillsone.com/pdfs/smp248148.pdf*

Heitler, S. (2012). *What Makes Conflict? How Are Conflicts Resolved?* Retrieved from http://www.psychologytoday.com/blog/resolution-not-conflict/201211/what-makes-conflict-how-are-conflicts-resolved.

Kilmann Diagnostics. (n.d.) *The Unique Benefits of Taking the Thomas-Kilmann Instrument (TKI).* Retrieved from http://www.kilmanndiagnostics.com/catalog/thomas-kilmann-conflict-mode-instrument

Leski, T. (2013). *Conflict Quotes: Conflict Resolution Quotations.* Retrieved from http://lenski.com/conflict-resolution-quotations/.

Noble, C. (2003). *Conflict Coaching for Leaders.* Retrieved from http://mediate.com/articles/noble3.cfm.

Swan, A. *How Do You Deal with Conflict?* Retrieved from http://icresolution.com/how-do-you-deal-with-conflict/.

Wilmont, W.W. & Hocker, J.L. (1998). *Why the Study of Conflict is important.* Retrieved from http://www.cios.org/encyclopedia/conflict/Asignificance4_advantages.htm.

Chapter 7: Style of Leadership

Hybels, B. (2002). *Courageous Leadership.* Grand Rapids, MI: Zondervan.

McIntosh, G.L. and Rima, S.D. (2007). *Overcoming the Dark Side of Leadership.* Grand Rapids, MI: Baker Books.

Sumner, Sarah. (2006). *Leadership Above the Line: A character-based leadership tool that leads to success for you and your team.* Carol Stream, IL: Tyndale House Publishers, Inc.

Williams, D. (1989). *The Art of Pacesetting Leadership: A Leadership and Ministry Development Course.* Lansing, MI: Mount Hope Books.

Chapter 8: Experiences

Fisher, D. (2010). *Our Daily Bread: What's in Your Hand?* Retrieved from http://odb.org/2010/11/29/what-is-in-your-hand/

Harlem Children's Zone (HCZ). (2009). *About Geoffrey Canada.* Retrieved from http://www.hcz.org/index.php/about-us/about-geoffrey-canada?id=400

Horn, J. (2013). *10 Secrets to Baking Perfect Cakes.* Retrieved from http://www.cookinglight.com/cooking-101/techniques/cake-baking-00412000067467/page8.html

McVay, D.A. (2001). *Drug War Facts: Comparing Addictive Qualities of Popular Drugs.* Retrieved from http://www.drugwarfacts.org/addictiv.txt.

The Rivard Report. (2012). *A Visit from Superman: Harlem's Geoffrey Canada Preaches Change to Fix San Antonio Schools. Were We Listening?* Retrieved from http://therivardreport.com/a-visit-from-superman-harlems-geoffrey-canada-preaches-change-to-fix-san-antonio-schools-were-we-listening/

Search Institute. (2004). *40 Developmental Assets*. Retrieved from http://www.scouting.org/filestore/pdf/40_Developmental_Assets_Search_Institute.pdf

TED Conferences, LLC. (2013). *Speakers: Geoffrey Canada, Education Reformer*. Retrieved from http://www.ted.com/speakers/geoffrey_canada.html

Chapter 9: Temperament and Personality

Carbonell, M. (n.d.). *What is DISC?* Retrieved from https://www.uniquelyyou.com/disc.php#Cdisc.

LaHaye, T. (1966). *Spirit-Controlled Temperament. (1st ed.)*. La Mesa, California: Post, Inc.

Littauer, F. (1992). *Personality Plus. (2nd ed.)*. Grand Rapids, MI: Revell Books.

Littauer, M. (2005). *Your Spiritual Personality: Using the Strengths of Your Personality to Deepen Your Relationship with God*. San Francisco, CA: Jossey-Bass.

Two-Factor Models of Personality. (2013, May 08). Retrieved from http://en.wikipedia.org/wiki/Table_of_similar_systems_of_comparison_of_temperaments

Warfield, H. (2008). *Sanguine: Outgoing and Disorganized*. Retrieved from http://introvert.cc/2008/03/sanguine-%E2%80%93-outgoing-and-disorganized/.

Chapter 10: Spiritual Gifts

Carraway, B. (2005). *Spiritual Gifts: Their Purpose and Power*. Enumclaw, WA: Pleasant Word Press.

Deffinbaugh, R. (2004). *"Spiritual Gifts (1 Corinthians 12: 1-11)."* Retrieved from https://bible.org/seriespage/spiritual-gifts-1-corinthians-121-11.

Great Christians in Business. (n.d.) *"RG LeTourneau – Earthmoving Innovator."* Retrieved from http://www.giantsforgod.com/rg-letourneau/

Hickey, M. (1986). *Know Your Ministry*. Denver, CO: Marilyn Hickey Ministries.

Ministry Tools Resource Center. (2013). *"What is a Spiritual Gift? A Biblical Definition."* Retrieved from http://mintools.com/gifts2.htm.

Spiritual Gifts Research. (2007). *"Spiritual Gifts and Personality"*. Retrieved from http://spiritualgiftsresearch.blogspot.com/2007/05/spiritual-gifts-and-personality.html.

Conclusion: What's Cooking—Where to Go Next

www.TheGodAssets.com

Bible Translations

Scripture quotations marked AMP are taken from the Amplified® Bible, Copyright © 1954, 1958, 1962, 1964, 1965, 1987 by The Lockman Foundation. www.lockman.org

Scripture quotations marked CEV are taken from the Contemporary English Version® Copyright © 1995 American Bible Society. All rights reserved. www.americanbible.org

Scripture quotations marked MSG are taken from *The Message*. Copyright © 1993, 1994, 1995, 1996, 2000, 2001, 2002.
Used by permission of NavPress Publishing Group.
www.messagebible.com

Scripture quotations marked NIV are taken from The Holy Bible, New International Version®, NIV® Copyright © 1973, 1978, 1984, 2011 by Biblica, Inc.® Used by permission. All rights reserved worldwide. http://www.biblica.com/

Scripture quotations marked NKJV are taken from the New King James Version®. Copyright © 1982 by Thomas Nelson. Used by permission. All rights reserved. www.harpercollinschristian.com

Scripture quotations marked NLT are taken from the Holy Bible, New Living Translation, copyright © 1996, 2004, 2007 by Tyndale House Foundation. Used by permission of Tyndale House Publishers, Inc., Carol Stream, Illinois 60188. All rights reserved. www.tyndale.com

The GOD ASSETS: God's Investment in You and What to Do With It